IAN COUTTS

Brew HOW North

★ CANADIANS ★

made BEER & BEER *made*

CANADA

GREYSTONE BOOKS

D&M PUBLISHERS INC.

Vancouver/Toronto/Berkeley

FOR STEPHEN ROSS WILCOX

A.K.A. SHOX JOHNSON

OCTOBER 6, 1955–JULY 17, 2000

. . . .

Greystone Books

An imprint of D&M Publishers Inc.

2323 Quebec Street, Suite 201

Vancouver BC Canada V5T 4S7

www.greystonebooks.com

Cataloguing data available from Library and Archives Canada

ISBN 978-1-55365-467-4 (pbk.)

Editing by Susan Folkins

Copy editing by Pam Robertson

Cover and text design by Naomi MacDougall

Front cover images: bear illustration by Talent Pun; beer photograph by John Sherlock

Back cover images © L–R: Library and Archives Canada, C 089660; York University Libraries, Clara Thomas Archives & Special Collections, Toronto Telegram fonds, 1821; Library and Archives Canada, PA 113191; York University Libraries, Clara Thomas Archives & Special Collections, Toronto Telegram fonds, 1820.

Printed and bound in China by C&C Offset Printing Co., Ltd.

Text printed on acid-free, FSC-certified paper

Distributed in the U.S. by Publishers Group West

We gratefully acknowledge the financial support of the Canada Council for the Arts, the British Columbia Arts Council, the Province of British Columbia through the Book Publishing Tax Credit, and the Government of Canada through the Canada Book Fund for our publishing activities.

FSC

Mixed Sources
Cert no. SGS-COC-003548
© 1996 FSC

CONTENTS

. . . .

WELCOME TO CANADA'S GOLDEN AGE

Looked at with the right perspective—through the bottom of a beer glass—there has never been a better time to be a Canadian. Look at the wonderful regional diversity: if you live in Toronto, you can drink Mill Street or Steam Whistle. If you live in Vancouver, Granville Island or Russell. In Montreal, Unibroue or McAuslan. Never have we had such beers to choose from. It's like multiculturalism in a glass: English bitters and German lagers. Live yeast beers inspired by the Belgians. Pale ales with an American west coast feel. And thanks to the big brewers, we even have beers that taste like nothing. You sometimes hear people talk about the good old days. Well, you know what? In beer-drinking terms, these are the good old days, right now.

Canadians have been making beer since the seventeenth century. And in that time, we have done pretty well out of it. Beer created some of our first fortunes and led the way to our nation's industrialization. It bankrolled

< *More truth in a single glass than in all the world's philosophy.*

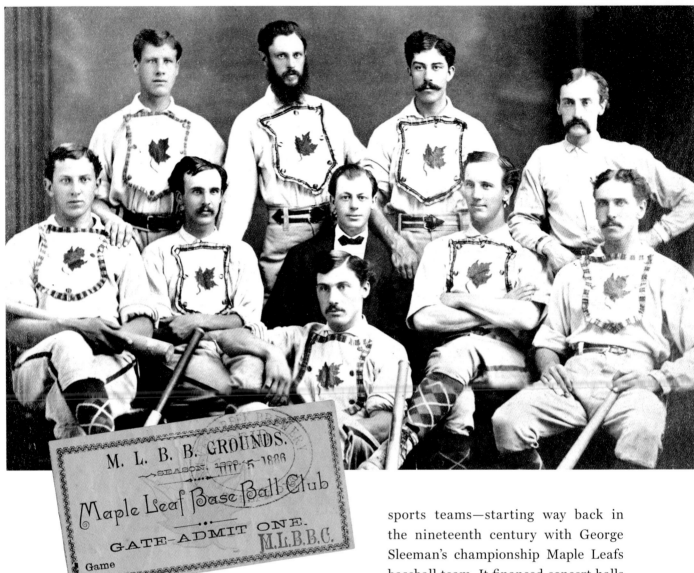

Sleeman's baseball team—the world "non-professional" champions of 1874.

sports teams—starting way back in the nineteenth century with George Sleeman's championship Maple Leafs baseball team. It financed concert halls and other public monuments, including Molson Stadium in Montreal and the Nova Scotia schooner *Bluenose II*, built with money from the Oland family's brewing fortune. To this day, you can't toss a stubby in London, Ontario, without hitting something named for or by a Labatt.

Socially, it's so important. While it's nice to think about the business side, we must never forget that beer is, first and foremost, a life-giving, health-some beverage, the drinking of which can strengthen social bonds, generate mirth, and enhance the workings of our minds. (It also makes others far

more physically attractive!) We may not drink more beer than anyone else in the world—the Czechs hold that particular honour, out-drinking us in 2004 by nearly two litres to one—but you know what? We drink an awful lot. We always have. In 2007, according to the Brewers Association of Canada, we put away 71.67 litres per capita (or 86.64 litres each, when those under fifteen, presumably never a terribly large part of the equation, are factored out). The Yukon led the way with a whopping 139.75 litres per capita, followed by Alberta with 98.54. Nunavut brought up the rear with 68.68.

When you learn about where we drank, what we drank, who we drank it with—and who tried to stop us from drinking it—you grasp a lot about this country's history and what makes it unique. Over the centuries we have slopped back dark porters in rough taverns, drunk India pale ale with one arm propped on a mahogany bar in classic Victorian saloons, and sipped 8-ounce draft glasses of frigidly cold lager in beer parlours that resembled

More than a beverage, beer is a food group unto itself.

Peter and Joey of Don Shebib's film Goin' Down the Road *drown their sorrows in draft.*

public washrooms. At times in our history, you generally drank your beer standing up; at other times, you could drink it only sitting down. In yet other eras, you couldn't drink it at all, or you found yourself restricted to an insipid near beer. And when it came to public beer drinking, women were often barred—or shunted to one side. Beer companies use an idealized version of ourselves to sell it to us (think: I AM CANADIAN). Writers and singers from Catharine Parr Traill to Al Purdy to Stompin' Tom Connors have eulogized it. Where would SCTV's two most memorable characters, Bob and Doug McKenzie, have been without their trusty two-four? And don't forget their movie, either—*Strange Brew,* a (very) loose retelling of *Hamlet,* featuring the two

Loyal and dependable, beer is one of our best friends.

CANADA IN THE MAKING. 1867. THE ORIGINAL TABLE IS IN THE SASKATCHEWAN LEGISLATIVE BUILDING

'67 BEER

FROM MALT AND HOPS   CONTENTS 12 FLUID OUNCES
THE SASKATOON BREWING CO. LIMITED SASKATOON, SASK.

hapless hoseheads battling Max Von Sydow for control of a brewery named Elsinore. Canadians made beer. And you know what? Beer made us. Just as much as the fur trade—hell, maybe more.

We need to appreciate this past, to imbibe, literally and metaphorically, our nation's liquid history. To learn what beer has done for—and to—us. Go grab a cold one, sit yourself down, and let's get started.

Like the Fathers of Confederation, beer helped create Canada.

1

JOHN MOLSON AND THE BIRTH
OF A CANADIAN TRADITION

I T TOOK a war to get beer really going in Canada.

Oddly enough, First Nations peoples, the original inhabitants of Canada, had no fermented beverage. Anthropologists tell us that this state of affairs is quite uncommon. These peoples were still largely nomadic, and those who had taken up subsistence farming *did* have a suitable source from which to make fermented beverages: corn. Meso-American people farther south in the Americas had used it to make an alcoholic beverage. But this knowledge does not seem to have travelled north with corn, and in the relatively brief time they had been settled and farming, early native farmers hadn't had time to discover fermentation.

Nonetheless, the first European settlers to arrive here after the founding of the colony of Quebec in 1608 came to a land ideal for beer making. The climate was far colder than northern Europe's, but still good for

< Canadian breweries used wooden barrels right into the 1950s.

{ 7 }

Getting brewing started in Canada was hard, but when it got going we took to it.

growing hops and barley. Their new home was also blessed with plenty of clean, fresh water—rivers and lakes full of the stuff, in fact. Many of the early European visitors to Canada commented on the popularity of water as a drink. They found this choice of beverage highly unusual.

Despite such promising conditions, brewing proceeded fitfully. Canada's first brewers were Louis Hébert and his wife, who seem to have brewed exclusively for their own use as early as 1617. In 1646, the Jesuits built a brewery at Sillery, near the town of Quebec, but it seems to have been exclusively intended for, as they say, their personal consumption. That same year Quebec gained another brewery called La brasserie de l'habitation, which kept up production for two years before it burned down. Another habitant, Louis Prud'homme, opened a brewery around this time in Montreal. It promptly failed.

It isn't that the people of New France didn't know how to brew beer—they did. But they just didn't drink it much. When it came to alcoholic refreshments, they preferred brandy, or the wines of their homeland. A favourite homemade concoction was something called *bouillon*, made by tossing a ball of bread dough into a pot of spiced boiling water, and allowing everything to ferment. History does not record its flavour.

Not just a gustatory quirk, the habitants' love of imported alcoholic beverages had serious repercussions on the colony. Financially, New France was a shambles. Dependent on one product, fur, which was notoriously vulnerable to fluctuations in fashion, and with only one customer, France, for its goods, the colony did not pay its way. Making a bad situation worse was the colonists' dependence on imported wines and spirits. Every year, according to Allen Sneath, the author of *Brewed in Canada*, 100,000 livres drained out of the colony to provide New France's two thousand residents with enough booze to make it through the long winter.

In 1665, Jean Talon, the first appointed Intendant (chief civil servant) of New France, arrived in Quebec. He was charged with the job of putting the foundering colony on a firmer economic base. Through the Conseil Souverain, an appointed body of local worthies, he had a 1,200-hogshead limit slapped on to the amount of wine and spirits that could be imported each year. A hogshead was a barrel holding about fifty imperial gallons, or 238 litres, so this worked out to around thirty gallons of wine and spirits per resident per year. If people wanted to drink more, assuming any of them were still standing, it would have to be beer.

Talon received royal permission to establish a brewery at Quebec in 1667, and ordered two large brewing vats from France. He encouraged farmers to plant barley and hops, and at his own seigneury planted six thousand poles of hops. (This essential flavouring agent grows like a vine up lines strung from poles. The flower is the part brewmasters actually use.) Before long, the brewers at La brasserie du Roi, as the new brewery was named, were busy

We had plenty of water—"free from drugs and poisons"—for brewing.

The arrival of ale didn't kill off spruce beer; you can find it in Quebec today.

producing beer—likely some sort of dark ale. More than that, they were actually exporting it, sending two thousand hogsheads to France's possessions in the Caribbean in 1671.

Talon's initiative, alas, was short-lived. In 1672, five years after being granted royal permission to open La brasserie du Roi, Talon's time as Intendant was up, and he left the colony. New laws allowed for greater imports of wine and spirits, and Talon's brewery was dismantled (though you can still visit the cellars of La brasserie du Roi in Quebec City today).

Other residents of New France took a shot at brewing beer after Talon, but none of their breweries survived for long. There simply wasn't the demand. Apparently, the habitants scattered along the shores of the St. Lawrence made a drink from spruce boughs, in both alcoholic and non-alcoholic forms. The fermented version was usually made of spruce boughs boiled with hops, to which the brewer added a sizable dollop of molasses, then pitched in some yeast and let it stand for a few days. Modern-day home brewers who have tried to make spruce beer describe it as having a flavour not unlike cough medicine.

Then, in 1759, the British Army under General James Wolfe defeated General Louis-Joseph de Montcalm's French forces on the Plains of Abraham outside Quebec. At the Treaty of Paris in 1763, Quebec passed permanently into British control.

This was a sad day for New France, and the hapless habitants, who now found themselves under the control of a people different from them in religion, culture, and outlook.

But on the bright side, it was a great day for beer and beer drinking: the land that would someday be Canada was firmly in the hands of Britain, one of the world's foremost beer-making nations.

PAINTED IN 1810, when the forty-six-year-old Montrealer was on a trip to London, the only known portrait of John Molson shows a successful merchant, dressed in bourgeois black. What's interesting is his expression. There's a play of humour around his mouth and his eyes, but if you know anything about Molson, it's easy to imagine that while he is looking at you, he's also looking past you—because just over your shoulder is an opportunity.

That's pretty much the story of Molson's life: spying opportunities and jumping in fast.

Molson was born on December 28, 1763, in eastern England's marshy fenlands, near Moulton, in Lincolnshire. The family were garden-variety English yeomanry—not aristocrats by any means, but members of the property-holding rural middle class. Molson's father died when he was just six, his mother two years later, in 1772. Ten years later, at the age of eighteen, Molson was on his way to the New World, bound for Quebec in the company of two of his cousins. Their passage was pretty typical as eighteenth-century sea crossings went—drunk captain, bad weather, leaky ship— but they arrived safely at Quebec City on June 25, 1782.

From Quebec City, the three travellers headed to Montreal. A fairly rudimentary town of about eight thousand people, at almost the edge of European settlement, Montreal offered real possibilities for an ambitious young man.

Molson had some money and could expect a larger inheritance when he turned twenty-one, but what he lacked was a clear idea of what he wanted

ABOVE: *John Molson.*

BELOW: *More than two centuries later, beer is still brewed on his original site.*

Men handling barrels in a British brewery's vast storage vaults.

to do. Yet by early 1783, Molson had made up his mind. He moved into the house of Thomas Loid, not far from St. Mary's Current, in what were then the outskirts of Montreal. Loid had constructed a square-log brewery there in 1782, brewing some fifty hogsheads of ale in his first year. Molson was to be his partner.

Neither man seems to have known anything about making beer, as Molson and Loid hired one John Wait to serve as brewmaster and general labourer. But the two business partners had something going for them that was almost more important than a personal knowledge of brewing: a market. In the quarter century since the conquest, Montreal had gained a smattering of English and Scottish emigrants. And they all drank beer. In fact, British soldiers were issued with an allowance to buy it. In the absence of any local producer, however, it had to be shipped from Britain at great cost. Selling for six guineas a hogshead, imported porter went for more than rum brought in from the West Indies.

The new partners and their assistant got to work in the fall of 1783. Their equipment must have been fairly makeshift—as were their ingredients. Thanks to a wet harvest, the partners couldn't lay their hands on enough barley, so they made do with wheat. Not that it mattered much. Demand was high; in the spring of 1784, they were again able to dispose of fifty hogsheads.

What happened next is a twist that wouldn't be out of place in a novel of the era. In June of that year, Molson sued Loid for 150 pounds and won an uncontested settlement. Then, on June 22, the sheriff seized some of Loid's "movable" assets and auctioned them off, the money going to pay Wait's wages owed. A few months after that, Molson still hadn't got his settlement, so the sheriff seized the land and the buildings at St. Mary's and held a second auction, on October 22, 1784. No bidders appeared.

We tend to think of lawsuits as acrimonious affairs, but historians believe that Loid and Molson engineered the whole thing as a scheme so that Molson could gain sole title to the brewery before his twenty-first birthday. (Molson continued to live at Loid's house while suing him.) On January 5, 1785, just eight days after he turned twenty-one, Molson took control of the brew house and the land it stood on. He was now in business for himself.

Molson, anxious to lay his hands on the bulk of his inheritance to finance his new enterprise, set sail for England in the spring of 1785.

In *The Barley and the Stream*, probably the best of all the books written about the Molsons, author Merrill Denison makes a good deal out of young John Molson's return to England, particularly the time he spent in London that winter. New industries were being born and old ones transformed. Particularly brewing. Five of London's more than one hundred breweries boasted an output of more than 500,000 gallons annually. The Whitbread brewery in Chiswell Street was famous for its "Porter Tun Room," which housed the vat (or tun) used for making porter. This massive space featured an unsupported vaulted ceiling that was exceeded in width only by Westminster Hall in the Houses of Parliament. Whitbread also boasted what was only the third of James Watt's new-fangled steam engines in operation in Britain, which the firm used to grind malt and pump fluids.

Molson learned the secrets of brewing from books, such as this one on chemistry.

Denison admits that we don't know whether Molson actually ever visited the Whitbread brewery. But what was happening in British brewing influenced him. To ensure brewing moved from quaint craft to modern industry in his adopted home, Molson would require a new approach.

That meant new technology, like the thermometer and the hydrometer (which measured the specific gravity of beer). It meant treating the brewing process differently, too. More science, less craft. In 1777, John Richardson, a British brewing theorist, had published his *Theoretical Hints on an Improved Practice of Brewing*, the first-ever attempt at explaining the brewing process in a coherent, systematic fashion. On April 5, 1786, when John Molson set sail again for Canada, he had a copy of Richardson's book tucked under his arm. Forget a traditional apprenticeship; Molson would learn his craft the modern way—from a book.

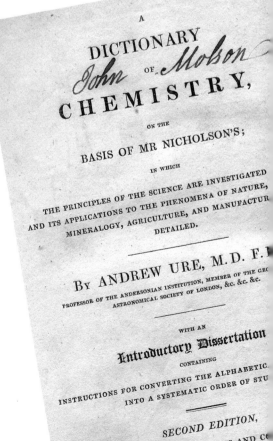

A

DICTIONARY
John OF *Molson*
CHEMISTRY,

ON THE

BASIS OF MR NICHOLSON'S;

IN WHICH

THE PRINCIPLES OF THE SCIENCE ARE INVESTIGATED
AND ITS APPLICATIONS TO THE PHENOMENA OF NATURE,
MINERALOGY, AGRICULTURE, AND MANUFACTUR
DETAILED.

By ANDREW URE, M.D. F.

PROFESSOR OF THE ANDERSONIAN INSTITUTION, MEMBER OF THE GEO
ASTRONOMICAL SOCIETY OF LONDON, &c. &c. &c.

WITH AN

Introductory Dissertation

CONTAINING

INSTRUCTIONS FOR CONVERTING THE ALPHABETIC.
INTO A SYSTEMATIC ORDER OF STU

SECOND EDITION,

OUS ADDITIONS AND C

Workers take a break from turning over germinating barley, used to make malt.

TO FULLY UNDERSTAND the revolution that Molson was going to bring about in Canada, we first have to understand what beer is. Not in the poetic sense, but in the more prosaic sense—that fluid in the glass before you.

At its most basic, beer features just four ingredients: water, yeast, malt, and hops.

The purpose of the water, as drinkers know, is to provide a socially acceptable distance between molecules of alcohol.

Yeast is a microscopic organism found in nature, and typically airborne. Yeast's secret is its ability to convert sugars to alcohol and carbon dioxide. People discovered a long time ago that, left on its own and allowed to go soft, fruit started to ferment. Mash this up and extract the juice, and you had a drink with pleasing properties. For this they could thank yeast—not that they knew about it. To them, fermentation was simply magic. For the longest time, most beer was what is called "lambic": the would-be brewer got hold of some barley, mixed it with water, left it alone, and *voila!* Beer.

Although lambic beer proved that grain—like fruit—ferments, kicking off the process takes a bit more work. Grain is protected by a tough husk, for one, which keeps yeast out. And it also contains not sugar, but more complex starches. This is where malting comes in.

MOLSON'S
Kamloops Hop Farm
LTD.

Malt starts its life as barley. To make malt, the maltster soaks the barley kernels in water. After immersion, the soaked barley starts to germinate—that is, sprout. This is a key step. Once the grain sprouts, it releases enzymes that begin converting the starches to sugar. In nature, the embryonic barley would use this sugar to push out of the soil.

But the maltster doesn't want the germination process to go too far, because that would use up the valuable sugars needed for fermenting. So after a few days, the maltster moves the germinating barley to a kiln for final drying. The kiln's higher temperature stops the seed from germinating any further. The brewer now has malt, a potential source of sugar for his yeast.

Once grown in Canada, hops are now imported from the United States and elsewhere.

LEFT: *To make wort, brewers heat water and malt in a large covered tank.*

RIGHT: *Once heated, the wort is pumped into a tank traditionally made of copper.*

Beer has been around for thousands of years (the ancient Sumerians were the first people to brew it, and the guys who built the pyramids were paid with it), and for most of its six-thousand-year history, it was made with just those three ingredients: water, yeast, and malt. The result was a sweet brew, much sweeter than we know today.

It was also much lower in alcohol, probably about two to two and a half percent by volume, and had what might be called a brief shelf life. These two facts were related. As fast as yeast could convert the sugars in the malt into alcohol, a bacteria of the genus *Acetobacter* was at work converting the beer into malt vinegar. Other bacteria attack beer, too, but *Acetobacter* is the worst of them because it actually consumes the alcohol. Early beer drinking was a race against time. What people drank was either too sweet or too sour.

So, welcome to the fourth of beer's principal ingredients: hops. Because early beer didn't taste terribly good, people flavoured it with herbs and spices. At some point in the ninth century, a group of German monks who were also brewers made an interesting discovery. Some hop flowers they had been fooling around with as a possible flavouring had an interesting side effect—they prevented the beer from turning into vinegar. For the first time, the yeast that

was producing alcohol could outpace the spoilage bacillus. This produced a much stronger beer, albeit one with a new bitter taste—what we think of now as the distinctive flavour of beer.

Once the brewmaster has his basic ingredients—and he can add others, for example, fruit, depending on the recipe—he sets to work. The beer brewing process hasn't greatly changed since Molson's day, and the steps involved are the same whether the brewer in question is making beer at home in a basement or at a vast factory. A good place to get an idea of what is involved is in a microbrewery or brew pub, where the equipment may be state of the art, but the human scale and time-honoured methods are not much different from those of two hundred years ago.

First, the brewmaster shovels ground malt into a large covered tank filled with water (commonly called "liquor" in brewing), which is then heated. This creates a mixture known as a "mash." During this time the enzymes in the

When the fermentation process is complete, the beer can be kegged or bottled.

17

Budweiser is Served at all First-class Hotels. Cafes and Bars

A beer so GOOD and of such UNVARYING QUALITY, boasts this 1906 Budweiser ad.

H ISTORICALLY, CANADIAN beer was always very different from the beer found in the United States. The reasons for the differences can be traced to major events in that country's history.

At the time of independence, Americans generally drank ale, like people in Britain and, later, Canada.

Beginning in the 1840s, the United States began receiving large numbers of German immigrants. Among these thousands of German immigrants were brewmasters, skilled at producing the lager beer that meant as much to the Germans as ale did to the British. Named lager because it had to be stored in a cool place during fermentation (lager comes from the German word *lagern*, to store), lager was a lighter colour than ale and lower in alcohol, too. Breweries sprung up all over the United States to produce lager for the country's burgeoning German population.

Before long, non-Germans were drinking lager too, often in charming beer gardens that were a pleasant contrast to the rough bars of the day. But two events really secured lager's place in American hearts.

Germans had been used to drinking on Sundays at home, and saw no reason to stop in their new homeland. They soon ran afoul of America's more puritan attitude towards alcohol. More than once, when the proprietors of taverns or beer gardens were hauled before the courts, juries ruled that they were not guilty because lager's perceived low alcohol content meant it was not an intoxicating beverage. The defendants produced witnesses who testified they drank lager daily with absolutely no ill effects. In one case, a man claimed to slosh down one hundred glasses a day while remaining stone sober. The idea that lager was not really booze boosted its popularity.

According to Maureen Ogle in her book *Ambitious Brew*, the rise in lager's popularity had some unintended consequences. Americans took to the German beers, but they approached drinking differently. For the Germans, beer was almost a food.

They wanted a heavy, nourishing beverage. For Americans, beer was a social beverage, and they wanted something lighter and easier to drink.

Smarter brewers started looking for a way to meet this demand. Lighter Bohemian lagers, such as pilsner—named for the Czech city where it was developed—seemed to fit the bill.

Unfortunately the six-rowed barley used by American brewers (Canadians and Europeans preferred the two-row type) was not particularly useful for producing these new pilsner beers. It wasn't until American brewers began combining their malted barley with what they termed "adjuncts" (typically white corn) that they started to develop a distinctly American version of such beers.

Foremost among these beer innovators was Adolphus Busch in St. Louis. Busch saw where American beer drinking was headed and in 1876 developed a version of pilsner beer using rice as the adjunct. Named Budweiser, the new beer was a light-coloured foamy lager that offered a uniquely American take on European pilsners. Thanks to Busch's marketing savvy, Budweiser became America's first national brand. Other brewers quickly followed his lead, creating light-tasting golden lagers that became the trademark American beer.

The mammoth St. Louis plant was the biggest brewery in the United States.

Dow Brewery was one of Molson's fiercest competitors.

malt get busy converting starches to sugar, which creates a fluid known as a "wort." From there, the wort is pumped to another tank, traditionally copper, and then brought to a boil. It is boiled for about ninety minutes, to sterilize it. Boiling also helps the hops, once they're added, to infuse the wort more readily. Then the beer is allowed to cool. Nowadays, it is pumped through a heat exchanger that lowers the temperature mechanically.

Once the temperature has dropped the desired amount—to about 20–26 degrees Celsius for ales and 10–14 degrees for lagers—the yeast is added (or "pitched"). The tank is sealed to prevent contamination, but fed with oxygen to encourage the yeast to reproduce frantically for at least eighteen hours, and then get busy converting sugars to alcohol. How long beers are stored after this varies according to what is being brewed. Stout might take only fourteen days or so before it is ready to be kegged or bottled. Lager will take much longer, months sometimes, at the cool temperatures it needs to complete fermentation. But ale or lager, stout or porter, at the end of it all those four base ingredients have been miraculously converted into drinkable beer.

ARRIVING HOME WITH his legacy—in the form of 175 pounds sterling, 46 bushels of barley and seeds, some hops, barrels, brewing equipment, and of course his precious book—John Molson took a while to get down to work. On July 28, 1786, he wrote in his diary: "This day bought 8 bu. of barley. MY COMMENCEMENT ON THE GRAND STAGE OF THE WORLD."

Molson worked alone at first, but by October, aided by a succession of assistants, he was brewing beer in earnest. All went well. "My beer," he wrote to one acquaintance, "is universally well liked, beyond my most sanguine expectations."

That first season, brewing for twenty weeks in the fall and winter (beer making was still tied to the harvest and the weather), Molson produced just over 4,000 gallons of beer. Some of this was traditional English ale, which Molson offered for three pounds, twelve shillings a barrel. In doing so, he undercut the price for imported porter, which at this point was fetching five pounds, five shillings. The bulk of his product, however, according to Denison, consisted of lesser brews with lower alcohol content levels. These were mild, table, and small beer, which were made with weaker mashes or by taking the mash used to produce ale and soaking it a second or even a third time to brew another batch. Table and small beer were very weak beers indeed, historically drunk in lieu of water, at every meal including breakfast, by everyone— even women and children.

As well as brewing, Alexander Keith had interests in banking and insurance.

A large part of Molson's market had disappeared when the bulk of the soldiers left Montreal with the coming of peace, but he had gained another: the United Empire Loyalists moving north in the aftermath of the American Revolution. Something on the order of ten thousand people made their way to Canada.

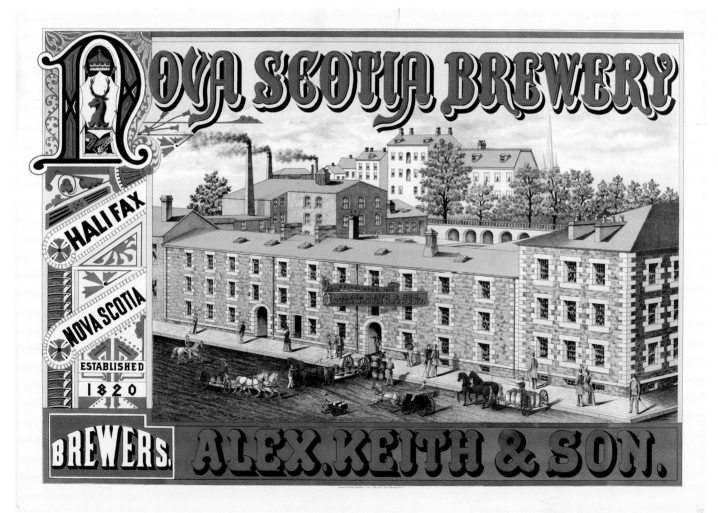

Susannah Oland (top) and John Sleeman (above, seated) both founded brewing dynasties.

With this influx, Molson never looked back. What followed was steady growth, verging at times on the spectacular. By 1791, he was selling 30,000 gallons of beer a year. In 1795, he constructed a new stone brewery building. In 1796, he "tunned" more than 54,000 gallons.

Always looking for the next big thing, Molson started to diversify. He began making small business loans to friends, a practice that would ultimately evolve into the creation of Molsons Bank in 1837. In 1809, he launched the *Accommodation*, the first steamship to sail the St. Lawrence. That one ship grew into a fleet of ships plying the river and Lake Ontario under the name The St. Lawrence Shipping Company (popularly known as "the Molson Line"). Molson had a hand in distilling, in running hotels—even, in the very late years of his life, in building Canada's first railway. John Molson not only kicked off Canadian brewing, he also initiated the birth of Canadian capitalism.

Diversifying was wise, because before too long he had competition in the beer business. In 1790, Thomas Dunn opened a small brewery across the St. Lawrence at La Prairie. His company would ultimately evolve into Dow, one of Molson's greatest competitors. In 1811, Thomas Dawes, who had trained as a brewer in England, opened a brewery at Lachine. These were just two breweries that managed to survive well into the twentieth century; there were many others.

The pattern repeated itself throughout the British colonies that would ultimately become Canada. In 1820, a young Scottish emigrant, Alexander Keith, bought out his boss's Halifax brewery and went into brewing ale on his own. Nova Scotia's redoubtable Oland clan set up in the same city in 1867, using Susannah Oland's home-brew recipes. In Ontario, John Sleeman opened his

brewery in St. David's, near Niagara Falls, in 1836. The year 1828 saw London, Ontario, gain the brewery that would ultimately be taken over by John Labatt in 1846, and Thomas Carling founded his brewery in that city in 1840, conveniently locating it across from the new army barracks.

Wherever there were Loyalists, recent emigrants from the United Kingdom, or military garrisons, you would find a brewery. Often brewing was one of the first industries in a new town, and the brewery owner was a respected local figure. Some of these men were brewers by training, but many were just like John Molson—guys looking for a lucrative business opportunity.

By the time of Confederation in 1867, a distinctive Canadian brewing tradition had emerged. We liked our ales and porters, and whatever their roots we saw them as distinctly our own. This was particularly true when we contrasted what we had in our mugs with what Americans drank. Now here was a truth *we* held to be self-evident. Our beer was stronger, tasted better, and was just all-round superior to their watery, pale concoction—heavily influenced by continental as opposed to British techniques—something no Canadian would dignify with the name beer. And although this tradition would weaken over time, it defined Canadian beer drinking for decades to come.

LEFT: *London's long-lived Carling Brewery was founded in 1840.*

RIGHT: *A Canadian brewery needed good water, soldiers, and Loyalists. Kingston had all three.*

23

2

"COME LANDLORD FILL A FLOWING BOWL"

OUR BEER-LOVING forefathers were not much given to solitary drinking. For them, the phrase "social drinking" would have seemed self-evident, a redundancy. Raising a glass of porter, pale ale, or (later on) lager was a profoundly public affair, to an extent we have lost.

This was so from the earliest days. Those hearty ales that John Molson and his competitors were turning out two hundred years ago weren't generally something you drank at home. True, Molson did sell some of his beer in bottles as early as 1800, possibly for domestic use. And we know that big, affluent households with plenty of family members and servants *did* order barrels of beer from him. Then there were the self-sufficient rural types, with barley and time on their hands, who surely made their own beer. But from the late eighteenth century to the eve of the First World War, if you were looking to down a few pints, you were looking to do it in the company of other beer drinkers.

< *The bar of Midland's Hewis Hotel boasted great decor and good company.*

Founded in 1795, this tavern in Hamilton was quite typical.

IN THE EARLIEST days, that meant leaving your rude homestead in search of a tavern. Fortunately, there were plenty of them. Walk any rutted road in the newly settled areas of Nova Scotia or New Brunswick, in Upper Canada, or the just-cleared lands of the Eastern Townships, and before too long you'd arrive at a rough-hewn log establishment set down in a stump-filled clearing, selling beer, cider, and hard liquor. In more heavily settled areas, you might find a handsome two-storey Georgian building, with a lovely fan window over the front door. Whatever the case, before there was a church or a school, there was always a tavern.

Historically in England the word "tavern" referred to an establishment that sold beer and wine, as opposed to an inn, which offered accommodation and meals. That distinction was lost in Britain's American colonies, where the words inn and tavern came to be used interchangeably—a practice that came north with the Loyalists. To be sure, you could get a drink (or several) at an

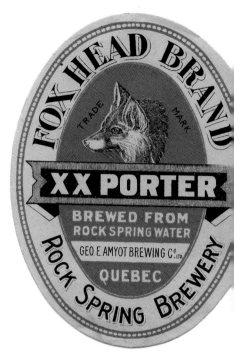

early Canadian tavern. But that wasn't its sole function. Moving along those rough early roads was a constant stream of settlers headed for new homes, farmers moving their produce and animals to market, government officials, and itinerant preachers and peddlers. Those early taverns, located every six or eight miles or so, and often built at crossroads, served as way stations, providing travellers with meals and a place to stay for the night.

Taverns played other roles, too. In the embryonic towns of the early nineteenth century, the local tavern did duty as a hiring hall, a town council chamber, a court room for the travelling circuit judge, an impromptu evangelical tabernacle, and a theatre. Lawyers and merchants used them to conduct business. Taverns were also good places to find out what was happening in the larger world. They often had the papers delivered by stagecoach, and there were always strangers around to give you the latest news. Circuses set up next to them. There is even a story of a coroner's inquiry being conducted

Historically, many Canadian breweries produced porter and its robust variant, stout.

at Butterfield's Tavern in Upper Canada's District of Newcastle in 1829, "upon the view of body of Esther Bradley then & there lying dead."

Not that the tavern's core business came to a halt when it was pressed into service as a public building. Far from it. There are tales of judges drinking while hearing cases, and at Freeman's Tavern in Chatham in 1836 a delegation greeting the then lieutenant-governor of Upper Canada, Francis Bond Head, was in such bad shape that many of them could remain upright during their audience only by leaning against the tavern walls.

ABOVE: Porter was popular in tavern days, but demand for it gradually dropped.

BELOW: This B.C. gold-rush era "Stopping House" eschewed such refinements as chairs.

Generally, though, no one went to a tavern to get drunk. They didn't need to. Plenty of general stores sold whiskey. Some would let you drink a dipperful for a few pennies (this was referred to as selling whiskey "by the grunt"). Others offered customers a few nuts for sale, their purchase entitling them to a "free" drink of whiskey.

Taverns generally didn't encourage drunkenness—that could lead to a reputation as a bad house, driving away more respectable customers and possibly imperilling the government licence they needed to operate. Drinking was a central part of life in those early colonies, but excessive public

drunkenness was frowned on. (In Upper Canada, at least, there were also what were commonly called "beer shops," which did not need to provide beds or food, and could not serve hard liquor. These seem to have been considerably rowdier and more disreputable. There were never very many of them, however, and they had pretty well disappeared by the middle of the nineteenth century.)

No, you went to a tavern for the people. Apart from the truly rudimentary frontier establishments, most taverns featured a separate barroom or taproom, often with its own exterior entrance. (Accounts suggest these were pretty much the same thing.) On entering, you'd find bare wooden floors and whitewashed, unadorned walls. Long benches lined the sides of the room, with perhaps a bare table in front of them. The bar would be in one corner of the room, the upper portion barricaded with what one writer described as a series of "palisados" (upright sticks or posts). A few of these could be raised or removed, leaving enough space for "three or four thrusting hands" to reach in and get their drinks. This arrangement allowed a landlord serving a full barroom to secure the booze if he had to suddenly go off and see to guests looking for food or lodging. (A bar in the sense that we use it, as a long counter, would not make its appearance much before 1830.)

Taverns were fairly democratic places. Once you grabbed your drink and crowded onto one of the benches, you might find yourself sitting next to almost anyone—a farmer, a travelling salesman, a soldier, or a merchant.

Taverns in towns, such as Toronto's Red Lion, had chairs, but not much more.

And, at least in the early days, this meant both men and women. Wedding parties frequently repaired to taverns to celebrate the happy unions. On other occasions, women would typically enter with their husbands or in large mixed groups. All-female tavern visits were certainly not unheard of, and women would even, on occasion, enter on their own. In her PhD thesis, University of Waterloo professor H. Julia Roberts mentions that Thomas Robinson, a tavern keeper in Prescott, Ontario, on the north shore of the St. Lawrence River, had two such clients recorded in his account book in 1847. One of these, a widow known only as Mrs. Wilson, seems to have been lodging at the tavern and during the course of her three weeks there, in addition to buying drinks for others and glasses of whiskey and brandy for herself, put away fifty-six pints of beer, an average of three a night.

What people normally drank varied according to what part of the country they were in. In Nova Scotia and New Brunswick, rum was widely available and was often mixed with water to make the ever-popular "grog." Lower Canada's French-speaking citizens still clung to their taste for brandy. Upper Canada's farmers grew more grain than anyone knew what to do with, and so locally distilled whiskey was popular there. But you would find beer pretty much everywhere. It may not have been the most popular beverage, but it was widely available and widely drunk.

In a tavern in a larger town you might drink ale from the likes of Molson or Dawes or Alexander Keith, or porter imported from England. Given the state of the various colonies' roads and the bulkiness of beer, however, these varieties weren't distributed very widely. A lot of taverns brewed their own. John and Henry Finkle, who in 1793 started up a tavern at Bath, just west of Kingston, Ontario, had the distinction of being if not the earliest innkeepers in the province certainly the first brewers and distillers. Margaret Simpson, who opened an inn near Belleville in 1810, also brewed her own beer. And there were other inns that can also be thought of as among the first brew pubs.

Today, we even have some idea of the taste of those early colonial beers, thanks to the intrepid English immigrant Catharine Parr Traill, who

Finkle's Tavern hosted Upper Canada's first criminal trial and hanging.

settled in Upper Canada in 1832. The author of *The Backwoods of Canada* and other works, Traill (together with her sister, Susanna Moodie, who arrived in Canada the same year) left us some of the best descriptions of the day-to-day experiences of the early pioneers in the new colony. Traill reported that the beer offered in those early taverns was very hoppy, "unlike the sweet, well-flavoured home-brewed beer of the English farm houses."

Beer would have been drawn from a small barrel behind the bar and probably served in a tin mug or glass tumbler. Glasses were relatively cheap in these colonies, unlike in Britain, where there was a tax on glass. By modern industrial standards, the beer wouldn't have been at all frothy, but would have had a slight fizz to it.

And it would have been served warm. By this time, British pubs, urban ones at any rate, were keeping their barrels cool in the cellar and drawing the contents upstairs by hand-operated pumps called "beer engines." That arrangement doesn't seem to have become common here until the final quarter of the nineteenth century. As the temperature of the tavern rose on a crowded, rowdy night, the temperature of your beer would have climbed with it.

How far a wagon could travel in a day defined a brewer's market.

Good or bad, you probably wouldn't have had a chance to order another beer before you discovered one of the tavern's most common customs: treating. This practice of buying drinks for others was known in Europe and the United States, but it reached almost epic proportions in this country. Writers from elsewhere frequently commented on how extensively practised it was here. John Moodie, husband of Catharine Parr Traill's sister Susanna, wrote,

> The practice of treating is almost universal in this country, and although friendly and sociable in its way is the source of much dissipation. It is almost impossible in travelling to steer clear of this evil habit.

A British settler, John Geike, also described the practice:

> Treating and being treated went on with great spirit, mutual strangers asking each other to drink as readily as if they had been old friends.

Horse-drawn sleighs kept beer drinkers tippling during the winter.

Apparently when you were treated, you took what was on offer. So you might well start out with beer, only to follow it, more or less willingly, with grog, a local pioneer distiller's idea of whiskey, any one (or more) of a number of sweet and spiced mixed drinks (with such names as shrub, sling, or toddy), or what was popularly called "hot stuff"—a punch made with whiskey.

Their drinks in one hand, their clay pipes in the other, the barroom's patrons sang the songs of England, Scotland, and Ireland (rousing tunes like "Come Landlord Fill a Flowing Bowl" or "The Beer-drinking Briton") or popular new tunes by the likes of the American Stephen Foster (though they probably skipped over his morose "Comrades Fill No Glass for Me"). Sometimes they made up their own melodies. People sawed away on violins. They discussed politics, though that could be touchy—some taverns had a reputation for being Tory houses, others for favouring Whigs. You wanted to be certain about that before you expressed an opinion on the Family Compact or the Rebellion Losses Bill. People fought in taverns, too. Sometimes seriously, in which case it was broken up fast or they were put outside, and sometimes for fun. Men wrestled or gave displays of fisticuffs. They took part in the long-lost manly art of "purring"—a kind of boxing with the feet, where two opponents, their trousers rolled up and their hands on each other's shoulders, kicked frantically at their adversary's shins. They might play cards, too, but probably for drinks, not money—strictly speaking, gambling was prohibited. And if the noise, the smoke, and the succession of drinks all became too much, you could always sleep it off in one of the tavern's lodging rooms—demand for beds frequently outstripped supply, so you might have found yourself waking up the next morning with one or even two total strangers as bedmates.

After the Second World War, the beer wagon evolved from a delivery vehicle into a marketing tool.

Joe Beef's Canteen, Montreal.

This popular nineteenth-century watering hole was described as "a den of filth" in the New York Times.

IN THE MID-NINETEENTH century, Canada started changing. From Britain's rag-tag collection of little colonies a new Dominion emerged, a land that would before long stretch from sea to sea, connected by the iron sinews of the Canadian Pacific Railway. More importantly, during these same years, Canadian beer drinking would be transformed.

Someone who had known only the rude colonial taprooms of the early nineteenth century would have been astounded by the changes. Gone were the unadorned walls, the pine floorboards, and the benches that were a feature of the taverns of yore.

Instead, a long mahogany bar dominated the room, which often boasted a floor of fine ceramic tile. Over the bar would hang a painting of a Rubenesque nude. The beer had changed, too. What you saw now in your glass was not muddy black or a deep brown but rather a relatively pale beverage, almost dark red in colour. Few, if any, customers drank it sitting down, assuming there were any chairs and tables. Instead, they crowded along the bar. Even the name had changed. This wasn't a tavern—it was a saloon.

There were a lot of reasons for the change. The railways killed off many of the taverns lining the country roads, which had depended on stagecoaches for their survival. As the country became more settled, the surviving old-style taverns lost their central place in daily life. A town that in 1800 had little more than a tavern would later in the century boast a courthouse, a town hall, a selection of churches, and perhaps even a theatre. Time was, the tavern had served all these functions. People now had more money and, relatively, more leisure time (though ten-hour workdays were common right up to the First World War). In the towns and cities where more and more people were living, they also had more ways to spend their money.

Victorian beer drinking was no laughing matter.

Smart tavern owners, the ones who as of the 1850s graced their establishments with the more raffish term "saloon," realized that if they wanted the public's custom they were going to have to work for it—become, as we say today, destinations.

Saloon owners here and in the United States took their inspiration from the latest wrinkle in English drinking fashions, the so-called gin palaces. You can still find them today in major English cities—London's Princess Louise, not far from the British Museum, is a great example. Inspired by establishments that had originally sold only gin, these were grandiose public houses, substantial and frequently multi-storey, featuring plenty of Victorian detailing on the outside, enormous windows (often of patterned frosted glass), and ornate mirrored interiors. They usually boasted a number of separate bars aimed at different classes of patron, and sometimes discreet, separate entrances for women. The main doors were often illuminated by elaborate gas lamps that lit up otherwise dark streets, drawing working-class drinkers like moths to a flame.

We don't have many written accounts of what their Canadian cousins were like. One

THE ~Lager SPLIT

Ales, like Molson's classic Export, were the eastern drinker's beer of choice.

SOME WAG (history has not recorded his name) once summed up Canadian beer preferences in this way: east of Yonge Street in Toronto everyone in Canada drank ale; west of it, everyone drank lager. This was an exaggeration, but it did contain a grain of truth.

Within the borders of Canada as it existed in 1867, we were strongly, if not exclusively, ale drinkers. The western beer scene was very different, however. Fritz Sick was arguably the most famous western brewer, a man who in his way was as important for brewing there as John Molson was in the east. Born in Freiburg, Germany, in 1859, Sick had trained as a cooper and coppersmith. Like many Germans of his time, he emigrated to the United States in 1883, and went to work in the brewing industry there, hitting the USA just as the truly American-style lagers were being created.

In the 1890s, Sick arrived in Trail, British Columbia, hoping to tap into a market of thirsty beer drinkers who had been drawn to the area by a mining boom. His first effort was short-lived, but he was more successful at establishing a brewery in Fort Steele in 1897. Selling his interest in that, Sick moved inland, fetching up in Lethbridge in 1901, and founding the company that would ultimately be known as Lethbridge Brewing and Malting.

Lethbridge's rail connections meant that Sick could ship beer to Calgary and other points, giving him a market larger than just Lethbridge's two thousand citizens. Sick's original beer, aptly named Alberta Pride, was a lager, and probably showed a strong American influence. Sick's firm survived the Depression and expanded throughout the 1920s and 1930s, opening plants in Regina, Edmonton, and Vancouver, and even moving into the American market. Sick brewed other beers, but lager was the company's backbone, specifically its Old Style Pilsner, which boasted what was probably the most beautiful label of any Canadian beer, a colourful jumble featuring a steam train, a biplane, monks, and what appear to be

Bronze Age men. It also bore the slogan "From the Cradle of Europe to the Rockies." At its peak, it was virtually the national beer of western Canada.

Although the most successful, Sick was not the only German brewer active in western Canada. Henry E. Reifel had a similar background to Sick's—he had emigrated first to the United States, and worked at a brewery in San Francisco before heading north to Canada. In 1888, he founded the Union Brewery in Nanaimo, which would over time morph into Western Canada Breweries Limited, a holding company that owned plants all across British Columbia and the Prairie provinces. The names of other storied western brewers, including Winnipeg's Drewry and St. Boniface's Kiewel, reflected their German roots as well.

Perhaps lager did better out west because of the presence of more German and (in southern Alberta, at least) more American immigrants. Or it may have been that thirsty pioneers were happy to have any beer to drink, and didn't mind if all that was on tap was lager. But whatever the case, lager, not ale, became the beer of western Canada.

Old Style's lovely label has not changed dramatically over time.

wonderful exception, however, was Joe Beef's Canteen in Montreal. Run by the eccentric Irishman Charles McKiernan, a former sergeant in the British Army who was popularly known as "Joe Beef," the canteen drew numerous journalists and others who wrote about it. One visitor writing about Beef's establishment in the *Montreal Witness* of April 4, 1881, described it as resembling "a museum, a saw mill and a gin mill jumbled together by an earthquake; all was confusion." Two skeletons, given pride of place behind the bar, served as handy props for McKiernan's tall tales—told in rhyme, no less. Customers shared the bar with a menagerie of animals, including a succession of bears, one of which, Tom, was known for his ability to put away twenty pints of beer a day. More than once McKiernan was mauled by his bears while encouraging them to show their ferocity. On another occasion, a run-in with a buffalo being displayed in the bar sent him to hospital for several days.

Thanks to the increasing commercial use of the new technology of photography, there exists an excellent visual record of those great Victorian saloons. They were overwhelmingly male places. As the nineteenth century wore on, the domestic ideal summed up by that old line, "A woman's place is in the home," gained a growing currency, not least among middle-class women, and they began to vanish from places where even a few years before their presence was unremarkable. A few bars did admit women, sometimes through a

For most of us, beer is the perfect excuse for good times.

separate entrance, but kept them isolated in a sort of state of alcoholic purdah. More than that, they were *young* male places. And even allowing for the more formal dress of a century or so ago, it's clear that these young men were working class: builders, factory workers, miners, cowboys.

For such men, typically bachelors and often working far from home, the fancy saloon was their answer to the tony men's club of the rich, a spot where they could gather after a day's work, to lean on the long bar with one foot propped on the brass rail.

The old taverns had served beer, but other drinks had provided plenty of competition. While the Victorian saloon invariably had a wide range of liquor bottles on display behind the bar, beer had become the preferred drink of its customers. Canadian beer consumption soared in the third part of the nineteenth century and into the early years of the twentieth, jumping from 2.2 gallons per capita in 1874, to 5 gallons in 1902, and 7 in 1913.

Fancy labels started appearing on bottles in the 1870s.

The same conditions that had created the new saloons, the railways, and urbanization were changing the Canadian beer industry. In his unpublished history of Labatt Brewing, Albert Tucker, a York University historian, now retired, described the change so: "In the 1860s, the company had been confined to a twenty-mile radius for sales and delivery beyond London," selling small barrels to rural inns and farmers. Just three decades later, "at least 65% of Labatt's Ale was shipped out of London by rail in puncheons containing 90–100 imperial gallons or hogsheads . . . the greater portion of this ale being delivered to bottling agents in distant urban centres."

As breweries sold more of their product indirectly through wholesalers and agents, and more of it in bottles, it became important to make customers aware of whose beer they were drinking. In other words, to have them connect with a brand. Beer bottles began sporting round labels, slapped on using flour paste. At first, they were simple one-colour affairs, giving the company name and location and the type of beer. But from the 1870s on they grew more colourful and elaborate, thanks to four-colour printing technology.

Dawes in Montreal used their trademark black horse on their labels, and Labatt adopted an arrowhead shape that was frankly an imitation of the famed red triangle trademark used by Britain's Bass Ales, which is the oldest-known beer logo in the world and is still in use today.

Labels weren't the brewers' only marketing tool. They had used advertising for a long time—Molson's earliest ad appeared in a journal called the *Canadian Courant* in 1807. But these ads had been simple announcements, just lists of products and their prices. At least as early as 1878, however, Dow Brewery in Montreal was placing something very similar to modern advertisements in the papers, featuring reproductions of their bottle labels.

Brewers also created a seemingly limitless supply of promotional materials to give away to saloons. London's John Labatt probably led the way in 1867, commissioning a picture of the company's brewery. Such pictures were popular bar decorations. In the decades to come, colour chromolithographs of breweries would form a virtual sub-genre of Canadian beer advertising, with the breweries depicted seeming to grow ever larger and more grandiose.

Virtually everything in a saloon could and did serve a promotional purpose. Your beer would arrive on a tray bearing a brewery name, and you might drop a few coins into the small enamelled metal tip tray also displaying the name of a popular brand. Lighting a match on a complimentary branded match strike attached to the bar, you flicked the ash from your cigarette into an ashtray bearing a brewery logo. There were bottle openers, coasters, foam scrapers, cigarette lighters, mirrors, calendars, clocks, paper fans, and more—all advertising breweries and their products, and adding to the delightful, anarchic clutter of Canada's Victorian saloons. In a sign of trends to come, many of these promotional giveaways featured pretty girls.

Marketing at times crept into murkier areas. At one point, according to Merrill Denison in his history of the company, Molson even supplied tavern owners with tables and chairs. In Ontario, at least, brewers went even further, making loans to saloon keepers to help them set up in business. It was a suspiciously grey promotional area, and there was some question about whether the breweries had crossed the line into ownership of the saloons—a bit like the situation in Britain, where for many years most pubs were "tied houses." Toronto's Robert Davies, owner of the Dominion Brewing Company, at one point also owned 144 taverns in that city.

THE BEER WAS changing, too, in the mid- to late nineteenth century. An increasingly sophisticated industry was ringing changes on beer's four ingredients to craft a wider range of offerings.

First off, consider malt. How long it is toasted, and how, makes a big difference to a beer's colour, aroma, and flavour. In days of yore, it was much harder to control the roasting process and most malt ended up being quite dark—giving English ales, for example, their traditional dark colour. Inky-dark porter, really the first mass-produced beer, used a lot of burned malt (and roasted non-malted barley, which was not taxed as heavily as malt), which gave it a special flavour, thanks to the caramelization of its sugars. In contrast, modern lagers like Budweiser and Canadian are made without any roasted malt—instead, brewers use a kiln-dried malt that is pale in colour. One of the

This handsome giveaway clock reminded drinkers that it was always time for Huether's.

Around 1860, India Pale Ale became the lead beer for Labatt and most other brewers.

42

most important developments of the eighteenth century was indirect kilning of the malt, which allowed the British to create paler ales, including the famed India pale ale.

Next, the yeast. Different strains of yeast produce different types of beer. For most of brewing history, the two most common types were top-fermenting yeasts, which produce ales and float to the surface when their work is done, and bottom-fermenting yeasts, which make lagers and sink to the bottom of the brew. Within each category exist many variations, producing markedly different beers. The nineteenth century saw a huge influx of northern Europeans—above all, Germans—into the United States, bringing with them their taste for lagers and the particular yeasts needed to produce them. This would ultimately have an impact on our beer, as well.

Hops are also quite diverse. This member of the nettle family (and close cousin of cannabis) is grown round the world—in Britain, the United States, Germany, and New Zealand, and can grow pretty much anywhere between 35 and 50 degrees latitude (though it is no longer cultivated in Canada). Different varieties of hops can be used to create particular aromas and flavours. The individual recipe dictates which ones the brewmaster uses. (The hardness of the local water may also play a role, as hard water brings out more of the hop's bitterness.) Cascade hops, so named because they are found in the Cascade mountain range in the western United States, are very popular in North America, particularly for the making of very bitter India pale ales, like the one produced by the Sierra Nevada Brewing Company. The United Kingdom has given us varieties such as Kent Goldings and the hop with the best name, Fuggles, both of which are used in many traditional British-style ales. Germany and central Europe boast the so-called noble hops, four strains commonly used to make lager.

These brewing innovations began to make themselves felt in Canada in the mid-nineteenth century. In an announcement that appeared in newspapers in the summer of 1859, Molson listed a variety of brands for sale, including India pale ale. That same year, John K. Labatt sent his son John (a favourite name, it seems, for Canadian brewers) off to Wheeling, West Virginia. He was to study for four years with George Weatherall Smith, an English brewmaster who had opened a brewery there. Smith taught the young Labatt the secret of India pale ale, or IPA as it was commonly called. Created for the export trade, IPA was intended to ferment slowly during sea voyages. The resulting beer had a high alcohol content, and the hops added to preserve it gave it a distinctive bitter taste.

People soon discovered that IPA had other attributes. By the mid-nineteenth century, glassware started squeezing tin, earthenware, and pewter mugs out of British pubs, thanks to the removal of the tax on glass. Beer had historically been about flavour and smell, but now drinkers could get a really good look at it as well. When they examined their popular porter, what they saw was a muddy, unappetizing beverage with what appeared to be silt floating in it. By contrast, IPA had a clearer, nicer appearance—not what we would think of as pale, but more of a pleasing, deep amber. And if it was more bitter than porter, it was stronger, too.

John K. Labatt seemed initially to have been interested in IPA's ability to travel—very much an issue in the Canada of the late 1850s. Whatever the company's reasons for starting to brew it, IPA was a commercial winner, and it would be Labatt's dominant brand from the 1870s until after the Second World War. The younger John Labatt, who took over the brewery in 1867, following his father's death, promoted IPA fiercely, entering it in brewing contests around the world, and then adding the brew's many laurels to the beer's label. Then, as now, there was nothing Canadians respected more than international validation.

IPA's popularity continued for several decades after the Second World War.

"MY DAUGHTER PUT IT UP WHEN SHE BECAME ENGAGED. THE NEW LABATT IPA LABEL IS HER WAY OF SAYING SHE'S GOT HERSELF A MAN"

John Labatt II brought the secret of IPA back to London in 1864. Winner of more awards than any other ale, it is famous as a MAN'S drink! Next time ask for IPA. If you enjoy an ale with that old-time flavour you'll like this man's drink too!

The swing is *definitely* to Labatts!

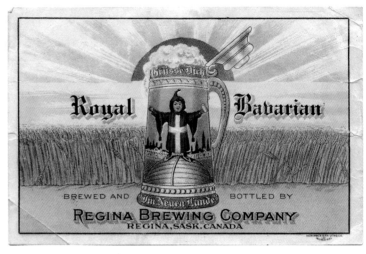

Lager—traditionally a beer of continental Europe—began appearing in Canada around this time as well. First to brew it seems to have been George Rebecher of Kitchener (then called Berlin), Ontario. By the late 1880s, Toronto's O'Keefe Brewing, which concentrated largely on producing lager, was one of the largest firms in Canada.

Even companies that stuck resolutely with ale were changing their brews. In 1897, as part of a series of moves by the younger generation to boost the family brewing business, F.W. and Herbert Molson modified the recipes for Molson's existing brews (though they balked at adding a lager to their line)

and added two new brands to capture changing tastes: Stock Ale and Export Ale. Of these, Export was the stronger and more expensive, retailing at $8.50 for a 25-gallon barrel, while Stock cost just $8.00.

The Canadian brewing industry mushroomed in the second half of the nineteenth century. To keep pace with the growing domestic demand for beer, industry production jumped 180 percent between 1873 and 1893, and overall production in gallons brewed rose from 11.6 million in 1874 to 56 million in 1914.

Despite the growth, Canadian brewing was a rinky-dink enterprise compared with the giant to the south. Those 56 million gallons were divided among 117 breweries, most of which, even large firms, had but a single brewing facility. In the United States, brewers like Schlitz and Pabst in Milwaukee and Anheuser-Busch in St. Louis had turned themselves into national powerhouses. They achieved this by developing bottling and filtration equipment and warehouses with state-of-the-art ammoniated cooling systems that extended the lifespan of their beers. The brew was then shipped cross-country in refrigerated railcars—the final stage of what was now a fully industrialized process and product.

"FRONTENAC
the finest on the Canadian market Made to compete with the
best imported beers"

*Before the First
World War,
regional breweries
thrived across
Canada.*

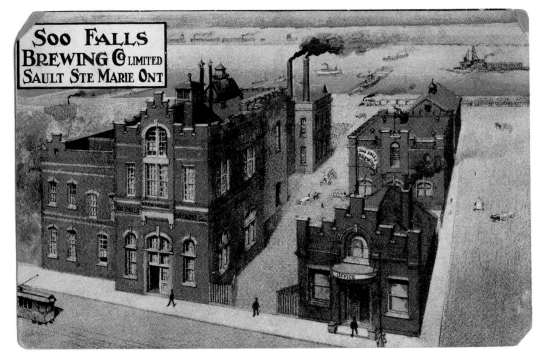

Canadian brewing was a far more humble, and haphazard, affair. Beer making now went on year-round, with the beer kept cool by enormous blocks of ice that had been cut from local lakes and rivers during the winter. It was bottled by sticking a rubber tube run from a hogshead of ale into the mouth of a bottle, and then slapping in a cork when it was full. Before use, the bottles were stored in crates packed with straw, a favourite spot for mice to nest. Alas, because ale bottles were dark green, the bottlers couldn't tell when one of them carried a furry passenger. That discovery would be made later on, by the prospective drinker of the beverage.

Though the technology was not sophisticated in Canada, it was a great time for the Canadian beer drinker. Stouts, ales, and lagers were all widely available. There were dozens and dozens of different breweries, and the products they made were all genuinely different. And then there were the saloons you'd drink them in—the *ne plus ultra* of public beer consumption.

GOOD BEER, GREAT surroundings, stimulating company—by the end of the nineteenth century, Canadians could be forgiven for thinking they were living in a state approaching brewtopia. But it was no picnic. Or if it was, it was menaced by a dark Calvinist cloud growing on the horizon. Or maybe by mean-spirited Methodist ants.

Around 1910, beer trucks began displacing horse-drawn delivery wagons.

47

3

THE LONG HANGOVER

L ET'S TRY a little experiment. Look back at those pictures of saloons in
the previous chapter. This time, try passing through the looking glass
and turning everything around. Try to see those various individuals not as
miners or factory hands or office clerks, but as vectors of poverty and despair.
Tell yourself that those saloons were not pleasant places to while away a few
hours, but menaces to the stability of the family and, indeed, to society itself.

On the eve of the First World War, this was an all-too-common view of
saloons—one held by more women than men, maybe, but not by a huge margin. The sooner the saloons closed and the spigots were turned off for good,
and the sooner those raffish layabouts gave up their carousing and started
trudging home to wife and brood with a full pay packet each week, the better.

By the early twentieth century, Canada's thriving temperance movement was already several decades old. It had been born as the offspring

< Toronto police arrest a man caught violating prohibition.

of two converging forces: the great wave of evangelical Protestantism that swept North America in the early part of the nineteenth century, and good old American self-help principles, advocating a temperate or moderate approach to drinking. Many of the early adherents to the temperance movement gave up only hard liquor (demon rum and rotgut whiskey), but thought that wine, cider, and of course beer were fine. They also sought to convince people to be temperate through moral suasion—moving first-person testimonials of lives redeemed, for example. They had some successes, managing to get many people to swear temperance oaths—10,000 in Upper Canada by 1832, 30,000 in Nova Scotia by 1837 (about 15 percent of the colony's total population)—but they had very little lasting effect. The taverns were still as full and the brewers and distillers still as busy.

The movement began to change in the late 1840s and 1850s. For people familiar with an older and more agrarian Canada, these were unsettling times. There was economic uncertainty. The Irish potato famine had washed a flood of desperate emigrants into Canada, many of whom were very different, culturally and religiously, from Canada's earlier English-speaking settlers. In the growing towns, a new working class was appearing, and its members often lived in conditions of desperate poverty. Temperance advocates were particularly concerned with the working man who squandered his hard-earned pay in some low saloon before staggering home to his defeated wife and their weeping, hungry children. In this unsettled world, as Craig Heron puts it, "booze worked well as an explanation for all the social ills of a society in transition to industrial capitalism." No booze, they figured, no problems.

Originally, when people "took the pledge," as they called it, they often took what was known as the "short oath"—swearing to give up only what they called "spirituous" liquors. Under this oath, it was okay to drink wine and beer. But because their entreaties had fallen on deaf ears, the movement decided no more Mr. Nice Guy. Now, temperance organizations began demanding that their members pledge what they called

Signers of this harsh triple oath swore off alcohol, tobacco, and profanity.

the "long oath"—forbidding alcohol of any kind. They referred to this as "total temperance," which gave rise to the term "teetotaller." They were going to rid society of alcohol completely. From their point of view, drinking could no longer be a matter of personal choice.

This sounds mean-spirited. It *was* mean-spirited. To rid the land of the demon rum, they would harness the power of the state. But rather than ally themselves with any one party, they functioned instead like a modern-day pressure group, working from the outside and putting the squeeze on politicians. In 1878, a group of teetotal MPs introduced the Canada Temperance Act, known as the Scott Act (after its sponsor, R.W. Scott). Under this federal legislation, any town or county could demand a vote on whether to outlaw the selling of liquor within its boundaries, and the results, one way or the other, could not be challenged for at least three years. In 1879, Fredericton, New Brunswick, became the first Canadian town to vote itself dry under the Scott Act. Over the next twenty years, many provinces voted in similar legislation that coexisted with the federal law.

Beer is dumped after Moncton voted itself dry under the 1878 Scott Act.

TEMPERANCE *Art*

Have You Any Boys?

At a meeting of the Ohio Liquor League a short time since one of the officers gave the following bit of advice to the members. It is quite in keeping with the diabolical nature of the business :

"It will appear from these facts, gentlemen, that the success of our business is dependent largely upon the creation of appetite for drink. Men who drink liquor, like others, will die, and if there is no new appetite created, our counters will be empty as will be our coffers. Our children will go hungry or we must change our business to that of some other more remunerative. The open field for the creation of this appetite is among the boys. After men have grown and their habits are formed, they rarely ever change in this regard. It will be needful therefore that this missionary work be done among the boys, and I make the suggestion, gentlemen, that nickles expended in treats now, will return in dollars to your tills after the appetite has been formed. Above all things create appetite."

HOW DOES THAT STRIKE YOU?

5000 PERSONS die off in Canada every year as the result of the Liquor Traffic. 5000 Boys are needed to keep up the supply. Have you any boys to spare for the purpose? As long as the traffic exists, they must be furnished. If you do not contribute, some other family must give more than its share. Is that fair?

If you think it is about time for this sort of thing to stop, mark your ballot thus :

Are you in favor of passing an act prohibiting the importation, manufacture or sale of spirits, wine, ale, beer, cider and all other alcoholic liquors for use as beverages ?	YES. **X**	NO.

Remember September 29.
Down with the Liquor Traffic!

PIONEER LIFE in Canada was a booze-soaked affair. It wasn't just that there were taverns in every town and at every crossroads, it's that alcohol played a central role in people's day-to-day lives outside the tavern, too: if you were a farmer and you wanted help raising a barn, you had to provide hard liquor if you expected anyone to show up and help. At the dances that were such a central feature of Canadian rural life, whiskey was as prevalent as fiddle music. People might have pledged to give up drinking, but it was hard to avoid in those rude settlements. The challenge was, as historian Craig Heron put it, to create "booze-free zones of sociability."

With that in mind, the temperance advocates set about to create a virtual "alternative culture" for their members. Central to this were the countless temperance organizations that encouraged people to sign the pledge, and also provided them with a new dry social network. There were numerous organizations of this type, including the Sons of Temperance, the International Order of Good Templars, and the Independent Order of Rechabites. (There were separate groups for women, too.) These were what you might term "dry" Elks or Masons: they held meetings and processions, they had ceremonies, and they often acted as benevolent aid societies, offering their members insurance and other benefits.

Another central goal of the temperance crusaders was to provide a more wholesome culture for their followers than they might have found in the taverns or at boisterous country dances. This new culture had the secondary goal of reinforcing the teetotal beliefs of its adherents and, functioning as propaganda, drawing in new members. There were temperance halls that provided dry entertainment, temperance illustrations like the ones shown here, temperance newspapers and magazines. Temperance advocates were avid pamphleteers.

In those early days in North America, music was probably the central popular entertainment, and temperance advocates were especially active in pumping out edifying sheet music. Although most of the songs were American, Canadians made their own contribution to the form with such classics as "Temperance Soldiers," "Father Sign the Pledge Tonight," and the ever-moving "Please Sell No More Drink to My Father," in which a child pleads with a local publican:

> He cannot withstand the temp-ta-tion,
> He feels when he passes your door,
> As he goes to work in the morning,
> Please, promise to sell him no more.

What is remarkable about this material from a modern perspective is its success. A case in point would be T.S. Arthur's classic novel *Ten Nights in a Bar Room*, in which an entire town basically drinks itself into ruin. It was eventually turned into a play that had the distinction of being the second-most popular drama in North America for most of the nineteenth century, beaten out only by a theatrical adaptation of *Uncle Tom's Cabin*. In a Victorian version of Hollywood screen adaptation, it was even made into a series of glass lantern slides that were popular at camp meetings all across the continent. Today *Ten Nights in a Bar Room* (in all its manifestations), and the torrent of other temperance material produced in the nineteenth century, is almost completely forgotten.

Anti-booze propaganda included pamphlets (opposite) and cautionary illustrations (above).

53

Beer's opponents were an unholy alliance of babes-in-arms and battleaxes.

Despite Fredericton's early plunge, however, surprisingly few other towns or counties seemed eager to take advantage of these new powers.

The impact on brewers was minimal. Even in those towns and rural areas that had voted themselves dry, beer was still easy to come by; the brewers, after a brief period of adjustment, suffered very little as a result of the Scott Act. To get beer to thirsty customers in towns or counties where the act was in force, brewers sewed quart bottles of beer into burlap sacks and then disguised them by packing them into barrels of flour. For beer drinkers, the Scott Act's most significant result was to hasten the transition in Canadian brewing from kegged beer to the bottled variety.

Still, as the nineteenth century gave way to the twentieth, temperance advocates, notably the powerful Dominion Alliance and the Women's Christian Temperance Union, scored an increasing number of small victories. They tightened the hours and days of operation (before 1900, in B.C. for example, bars were open year-round, twenty-four hours a day), and reduced the number of saloon and liquor licences. It hadn't been respectable for women to enter bars for decades; some jurisdictions now specifically banned them, as both employees and customers. Boxing, pool, and other pastimes were outlawed in bars. In Ontario, bars were obliged to close by 7:00 PM on Saturday nights. In Quebec—sensible, sane Quebec—a provincial government commission went so far as to suggest in 1913 the abolition of the saloon's trademark stand-up bar. More areas of the country were voting themselves dry via local option, too. Even swaths of rural Quebec opted for prohibition. Perhaps the greatest victory of the temperance movement, however, was a largely psychological one: they managed to stigmatize drinking, to put the fellow who enjoyed his beer, and the formerly respectable worthy who made it, on the defensive.

Yet the great glittering prize—to rid society of alcohol completely—still eluded them. Alcohol, however hemmed in by social disapproval and state regulation, remained legal in most parts of Canada. (Only Prince Edward Island went completely dry, in 1901.)

Further complicating the temperance gang's quest for a booze-free Dominion was an 1896 ruling in London, England, by the Judicial Committee of the Privy Council (then Canada's highest court). They may have been British, but when asked to figure out what level of government controlled the liquor trade they came up with a typically Canadian jurisdictional mishmash: the provinces had sole control over the retailing of alcohol, whereas the federal government enjoyed jurisdiction over its production and interprovincial export. There would be no simple solution to the problem of booze. The saloons stayed open and beer continued to pour from the taps. At least until the First World War began.

Canadian soldiers bound for France get their beer ration aboard a troopship, 1916.

IT TOOK THE Seven Years War, which brought Quebec under the sway of the beer-drinking nation of England, to get brewing really going in Canada; the First World War nearly finished it off.

This was war on an industrial scale, *total* war, involving not just soldiers but everyone—civilians, women, and children. For the first time in Canadian history, the government took on a big role in day-to-day life, stepping in to control prices and manage the food supply. "Duty" was in the air. The idea took root that, perhaps in these times of sacrifice, drinking beer and booze wasn't the best use of scarce resources. Now it wasn't just women named Nelly and Agnes from the WCTU or tight-lipped Baptist parsons demanding an end to the booze trade. Prominent businessmen and patriotic citizens called for it too, at least for the duration of the war.

Saskatchewan was first to go dry as a wartime measure. In 1915, the province closed all bars and liquor stores (though production remained legal), and restricted sales of alcohol to government stores. (Even these would close after a plebiscite a year later.) Next up were Alberta and Manitoba, where the issue was put to voters that same year, followed by British Columbia in 1916. The remaining provinces didn't bother with asking the electorate. Ontario went dry in March 1916. Nova Scotia and New Brunswick followed soon after. Both Ontario and New Brunswick would hold votes to extend prohibition after

Treasure greater than gold—a beer from town to town through wartime Toronto.

the war, with the dry forces succeeding in both cases. Only Quebec dragged its heels, announcing early in 1918 that it would enforce provincial prohibition—beginning in May 1919. In the meantime, bars and liquor stores could remain open.

Under prohibition, it was still legal for brewers to produce beer but they couldn't sell it locally. For their local markets, brewers were stuck making what was known as temperance beer, a beverage boasting a mighty 2.5 percent alcohol by proof (or about 1.5 percent by volume). They could still brew full-strength beer, but only for export to other provinces, a trade that was then under federal control. This led to some tricky juggling. Labatt, for example, set up an office in Hull, which took orders from Ontario, and then directed customers to pick up their beer from bonded warehouses in Toronto, London, or Hamilton. In December 1917, Sir Robert Borden's newly elected Unionist government closed this last remaining loophole. By Order in Council, all imports of alcohol into Canada ceased immediately as of March 1918; from April 1918 on, the production of alcohol was to stop and the interprovincial trade to halt. This new federal law was to remain in force for a year after the war's end (until November 11, 1919, as it turned out). Canada was totally dry.

Mercifully, this period of full-bore, out-and-out prohibition lasted only nineteen months. That said, those hard years between 1916, when most provinces had closed down their saloons, and 1919, when the federal ban on production came off, killed literally dozens of breweries. Of the 117 breweries operating before the war, 67 were wiped out. Ontario had boasted 49 in 1915; by 1917 only 29 of these remained, however precariously, in business. London's Carling hung on until 1920. Other venerable Ontario breweries, such as Kuntz in Waterloo and British American in Windsor, survived but never fully recovered. Saskatchewan lost three of its four pre-war breweries. The laws killed countless free-standing saloons and hotels that had survived on their barroom trade, too.

No doubt the temperance people were pleased with themselves. But strangely, almost as soon as prohibition was put in place it began to unravel.

Temperance beer predated prohibition—though it probably found few takers.

This Ontario brewery was one of many killed by prohibition.

The federal government had not extended its wartime ban on alcohol production, as the teetotallers had hoped. Wisely, prohibition or not, the government had never cut off the rum ration to soldiers serving in the trenches, and these returning heroes didn't much care for what they found on their arrival home. Returned soldiers' associations soon began actively agitating for prohibition's repeal.

Quebec had embraced prohibition very reluctantly, and had allowed for a long lead time before it took effect. Given a breathing space, Quebec's brewers launched one of Canada's first public relations campaigns. They ran ads in English- and French-language newspapers. "Is the Oldest Manufacturing

Silver Creek (left) and Rock Brewery (below) were other victims of the ban on booze.

Business in Canada to be Legislated out of Existence?" they asked. They created a Beer and Wine Committee, which they packed with prominent francophones to appeal to the most anti-prohibition constituency. In March 1919, the Quebec government agreed to a referendum on whether to exclude beer from prohibition, to be held on April 10. It passed by a huge margin. And when federal prohibition lapsed late in 1919, Molson, Frontenac, and Quebec's other beer makers went right back to brewing and selling their product locally.

Elsewhere, brewers did what they could to survive. There was the aforementioned temperance beer, which wasn't terribly popular. Toronto's O'Keefe and others turned to soft drink production. The Saskatoon Brewing Company turned out a non-alcoholic drink called Malta, presumably derived from malt. Beer drinkers, too, made do. Under provincial prohibition it was legal to possess full-strength beer, though you couldn't buy it, so many people brewed their own. You could also get alcohol by prescription, but most accounts suggest that people took this route to buy hard liquor.

For many Ontario breweries, their salvation proved to be, strangely, even more prohibition. On January 16, 1920, the National Prohibition Act, commonly known as the Volstead Act, came into force in the United States. This was a federal act, backed by a constitutional amendment, and far more rigorous than Canada's patchwork approach to prohibition. (Americans referred to prohibition as "The Noble Experiment." Compared with it, what we had was more like "The Noble High School Science Project.") The U.S. government banned not only the sale and public consumption of alcohol but its production as well. (Buying and possessing it remained legal.) As in Canada, numerous American breweries closed down, and those that stayed alive limped along any way they could, producing near beer, soft drinks, or, in the case of Stroh's and a few others, ice cream. (All that fancy refrigeration equipment they used to brew lager came in handy.)

Canadian brewers and distillers, of course, were permitted by law to maintain production even if they couldn't sell the output locally. One province could export it to another province or to another country. When it came to foreign exports, the Canadian government was concerned only that the excise tax be paid, and that the proper export form, the B-13, be filled out. Beyond that, they essentially turned a blind eye. Canadian alcohol exporters (to give bootleggers a fancier name) typically wrote down Cuba, Bermuda, or some other distant island as their destination—even when they were shipping the booze from the north shore of Lake Erie or rowing it through the Thousand Islands in a skiff. No one was fooled, but no one said anything, either.

By far the biggest conduit of Canadian alcohol into the United States was through southwestern Ontario into Detroit and from there on to Chicago and the parched American Midwest. Bootleggers found it more profitable to smuggle whiskey, but lots of Canadian ale and lager found its way into the United States too. Eighty percent of it flowed across the border at and around Detroit.

One of the first firms to take advantage of this new market was London's Labatt Brewing. Promising the family that he would operate within the constraints of the Ontario Temperance Act, company manager Edmund Burke created a distribution network to get their product into the United States (including a new beer created in the 1920s for the export market, Labatt's Crystal Lager). Burke rented warehouses convenient to the docks in Ford City near Windsor, Port Stanley, and Sarnia. He purchased boats to run Labatt's beer into the United States. He even found a way to load beer surreptitiously onto American trains cutting through Canada between Michigan and upstate New York.

Others followed Labatt's lead. Ontario's brewers had always been careful about stepping on one another's toes, avoiding costly price wars, and now they brought that spirit of collusion to their bootlegging trade. Eleven Ontario breweries, Labatt and Carling among them, banded together to export beer to the United States, agreeing on prices and dividing up market share. Two years later, in 1926, they became a formal cartel under the name the Bermuda Export Company. (It is highly doubtful any of their product ever reached Bermuda.) They set the price of a case of twenty-four pint bottles at $3.25 and selected a limited number of agents to act for them in the United States.

It may be surprising, but Quebec's brewers, who were also near major American markets and had the added advantage of being able to legally produce and sell beer, don't appear to have taken advantage of their situation the way that Ontario's did.

According to Merrill Denison, chronicler of the Molson saga, they were aware of just how fortunate they were to be able to carry on their business legally, and did not want to give the government any reason to act against them. Besides, they need hardly have bothered with smuggling. By the early 1920s, as the only wet jurisdiction in the eastern half of North America, Quebec, and Montreal especially, started drawing plenty of tourists from the northeastern United States and Ontario, eager to experience La Belle Province's charms first-hand, especially while holding a bottle of Black Horse or Stock Ale.

You might wanna beer, but as the label let you know, you weren't going to get it.

Prohibition in Canada was, to put it mildly, a farce. People felt free to ignore it—even some who had voted in favour of it. How could that be? Perhaps Stephen Leacock explained the seeming paradox best in his 1919 article "The Tyranny of Prohibition," written to warn the people of England against the dangers of the temperance movement. There were, he said,

great numbers of people in favour of prohibition for everybody except themselves... The manufacturer voted his employees dry... proposing for himself to remain "wet." The shopkeepers of the town voted the farmers dry so as to get more money in trade. The farmers who live in the country where it is dark and silent, helped to vote the cities into dryness as a spite against their lightness and gayety.

Watching how poorly prohibition worked, and alarmed at the breakdown of respect for the rule of law, people began to turn against it. Governments were also becoming aware that a roaring illegal liquor trade was an untaxed one. Quebec of course had barely had prohibition at all, and B.C. had gone wet again in 1921. The rest soon followed, with only Prince Edward Island, the first province to go dry, holding on throughout the 1930s and the war, becoming wet again only in 1948.

Plenty of breweries were ready to start selling when their province's laws were repealed. Labatt in London had already developed a surreptitious local trade to complement their booming export business. Among other scams, they sold full-strength beer packed in temperance beer boxes to trusted customers. When prohibition was lifted in Ontario they were producing full-strength beer at 90 percent capacity. Selling beer to the Americans had been so good for the company they had actually grown during the years that the

During prohibition, the Olands survived, even thrived.

Ontario Temperance Act was in force, expanding from 68 employees in 1922 to 104 by 1925. Oland Brewery in New Brunswick had been producing full-strength beer since 1924, selling it to local stores and other outlets, and then helping cover businesses' fines when they were charged under the law. Between 1924 and 1926, the company shelled out $24,000 in this way, recording the amounts in their books as travel expenses, wages, and salaries. Expensive, but it kept their beer out there and sustained a demand that could only grow once prohibition ended.

But when Canadians at long last sat themselves down for a drink in their local watering holes, they discovered that the taps were flowing in a very different world, beer-wise.

4

ABANDON HOPE,
ALL YE WHO ENTER HERE

THE END of prohibition didn't mean an immediate return to the good old days. The temperance people may have lost the war, but they still managed to ruin the peace. Alcohol retained its stigma, and has to this day. The watchword became not prohibition but *control*. The provincial governments would have a monopoly on the sale of alcohol. (Allowing, that is, for another typically Canadian mish-mash: Quebec would allow grocery stores to sell beer and, later, wine. In Ontario, the government liquor stores found it too much trouble to handle beer, so they fobbed the job off on the brewers, who sold it through their highly profitable Brewers Warehousing outlets. In western Canada, in addition to selling beer by the glass, hotels could also sell bottled beer for off-premise consumption.)

In every province except Quebec and New Brunswick, ordinary citizens needed a permit, renewable annually, to buy from the provincial

< *Draft beer sirens from a Winnipeg beer parlour of the early 1960s.*

Quebec was easy on beer buyers; Ontario and other provinces made it hard.

liquor store. These permits were usually small booklets in which the store clerk would record the dates and amounts of your purchases. Be seen as buying too much, and you could lose your permit. Native Canadians were denied permits altogether. Some provinces set quotas on how much you could buy: two dozen quarts a week was the beer limit in Manitoba, while next-door Saskatchewan set it at two gallons.

Right after prohibition was lifted, the only place you could have a drink was at home. Possibly fearful of the temperance movement, which was far from a spent force, no one in government wanted to be seen as supporting a return to the days of the "wide-open saloon." (If, indeed, the saloons ever really had been as "wide open" as their detractors claimed. One of the problems with the history of drinking in Canada is that most of the accounts we

have are the hardly unbiased reports of people who wanted prohibition. It's a rare instance of history's having been written by the losers.)

But as province after province approved the sale of alcohol, pressure mounted for the sale of beer by the glass. The voices of sanity were particularly strong among veterans' organizations and the blue-collar men who had patronized the pre-prohibition saloons. Quebec okayed the move in 1921, and British Columbia approved it in a referendum in 1925. Other provinces followed suit within a few years of abandoning prohibition, though Nova Scotia held out until 1948 and New Brunswick forbade public drinking until 1961.

When it comes to public beer drinking, there are several possible models. Germany gave the world the beer hall, where portly Teutons in leather shorts link arms and sing as buxom blond barmaids slam down giant steins of lager. England gave us the pub, with its warm brown beer and its pleasant fug of pipe tobacco and the old Lab sleeping by the fire. The United States gave us

You had to experience a beer parlour to really understand it.

Beer parlours were a deliberate, sombre negation of the old-style saloon.

the neat little neighbourhood bar, with its neon beer signs in the window and a great jukebox, a place "where everybody knows your name." All of these models have been picked up and imitated worldwide.

Canada gave the world the beer parlour. But no one seems to have emulated us. No one in their right mind would have wanted to.

Talk to anyone old enough to remember what it was like to drink in Canada's old-school beer parlours, the kind that dominated our beer landscape from the 1930s to the 1970s, and you'll hear a lot of "d" words. Draft, for starters, which is what everyone drank. Not, it seems, draft ale or draft lager, just *draft*. Then they might say dingy, which pretty well sums up the places where they knocked back that beer. Finally they could bring up dingy's close cousin, depressing, which was the overall effect of the experience.

One last "d" word needs to be added: *deliberate*. Those unlamented beer parlours, oppressive to the nation's beer drinkers and ridiculed by any foreigner unfortunate to set foot in one, were no accident. They were a conscious piece of social engineering, on a par (at least to any right-thinking beer drinker) with Mao's Cultural Revolution or Lenin's bid to create the new Soviet man.

Essentially, what the country's new liquor boards set out to create could be thought of as the "anti-saloon." To create it, regulators took all the qualities of the original saloons and came up with their opposite. The saloon featured a long bar lined with beer taps and a handsome brass foot rail; the beer parlour featured no bar. (Indeed, in the initial British Columbia plebiscite on beer by the glass, voters were asked whether they approved its sale "in licensed premises *without a bar*.") In its place was a small counter or even a large square pass-through in the wall, called a service counter, with the beer kept out of sight behind it. To one side of this counter hung a series of small signs

At beer parlours everywhere, mingy, off-limits service counters usurped lovely old bars.

ABOVE: *A waiter in a Montreal tavern in the 1960s races draft beer to his customers.*

BELOW: *Brewery giveaways—and posted regulations—were the sole decor at beer parlours.*

listing what beer was on tap that day. Rather than standing at the bar, the patrons now sat four to a table, each table featuring a salt shaker (to add salt to the beer) and an ashtray. A waiter brought patrons their beer; they could not order a drink and bring it back to their table. Nor could they take their drink and move to another table. In fact, they couldn't stand up with their drink. The painted nude that had once hung over the old saloon bar was gone, as were most other forms of decoration, save perhaps for a few small pictures, some beer company giveaways, and various prominently posted regulations. Windows were almost completely bricked up or fitted with heavy green curtains. Even the names were tightly regulated. People may have called them beer parlours informally, but outside of Quebec, where the word "tavern" was used, owners were prohibited from referring to their businesses as bars or saloons or making any too-obvious reference to their function. They were usually known officially as "beverage rooms."

"Beverage" meant "beer," of course. Generally, nothing but beer was available (though Ontario, at least, did permit the sale of wine). Moreover, maybe because it was served by the glass, draft beer was the bedrock of beer parlour

70

consumption, doled out in uniform 8-ounce glasses that featured a prominent line showing how full the glass should be. In fact in 1926, their first year of full operation, Vancouver's beer parlours went through 70,000 barrels of draft, and the equivalent of just 10,000 barrels of bottled beer.

Always an innovator, Labatt created a special service division in 1935, after beer by the glass became legal in Ontario, to help hotels with installing and servicing the equipment they needed to serve draft beer. Draft's hold began to weaken only during the Second World War. Beer parlour owners, responding to shortages brought on by the war effort, surreptitiously tried to stretch their supplies by reducing the amount of draft they poured into a glass, usually by letting the head foam up over the pour line.

True beer parlour aficionados ordered their draft by the trayful.

The beer parlour was created as the solution to a problem—the saloon. But for those who regulated them, almost every possible human behaviour

Ladies AND Escorts

ONE WAY that the new-fangled beer parlours were actually an improvement on the old saloons was the presence of women. They weren't allowed everywhere—Saskatchewan, Manitoba, and Quebec all barred them, though women in Quebec could drink in public in cafés and elsewhere. But they were allowed through the doors of beer parlours in British Columbia, Ontario, and Alberta, and ultimately the Maritime provinces as public drinking opened up there. (Actually, Alberta banned women from parlours in Calgary and Edmonton and let them drink only in special segregated rooms elsewhere in the province.)

A well-dressed patron enjoys the restrained ambience of the Ladies and Escorts *room.*

British Columbia and then Ontario, following on its model, added separate rooms within the beer parlours, where women could drink alone, in groups, or with their male companions—from whence came the name given these draft beer seraglios, "Ladies and Escorts." Certainly some women had always drunk at home. But by driving male drinking out of the saloons and then initially limiting legal consumption to the home, the temperance movement and prohibition probably exposed more women to the pleasures of beer and social drinking. Thus it made sense that when men tramped off to the newly opened beverage rooms, the womenfolk would follow. Changes in attitude about women and their role in society also made a difference.

For the fussy puritans who controlled Canadian drinking in those days, the presence of women of course created regulatory problems. The lone woman who entered the Ladies and Escorts section might be a prostitute, there to troll for customers. More common, but no less annoying, were what were called in British Columbia "crossovers" and "wandering"—crossovers were lone men who attempted to literally cross over from the Men's Only to the Ladies and Escorts area; wandering referred to the tendency of some men, having eased their way into the Ladies and Escorts section, *sans* lady, to move from table to table of women all night—not very escortly behaviour.

Male-only company could be dull, but you need never take your hat off.

represented a potential problem. People wanted to dance. Nip that and they started to sing. Stop them from singing and they wanted recorded music. You can get an idea of just how zealous the regulations were from Craig Heron's article "The Boys and Their Booze," which appeared in *The Canadian Historical Review* in September 2005. Heron quotes a reply from the Liquor Control Board of Ontario to a Hamilton-area hotel that asked permission to install a "music machine" (presumably a jukebox) in the dining room adjacent to the beer parlour:

> ... the machine shall at all times be played softly [so as not to be heard in a beverage room] and if at any time the dining room is used as an overflow beverage room the machine must be absolutely disconnected and not allowed to be played.

One wonders: why give away songbooks? You couldn't sing in a beer parlour.

The ultimate paradox of the beer parlour was that the rules were there to curb excessive drinking, but as Robert Campbell puts it in his wonderful book *Sit Down and Drink Your Beer*, "the irony of these restrictions was that in a beer parlour there was little to do except drink."

Yet despite the gloomy surroundings, the welter of restrictions, and the general atmosphere of disapproval, people got on with having a good time as best they could. They talked and argued, they bought one another drinks. W. Edward Mann, an Anglican minister and academic, penned this positive description of beer parlour life in Toronto's Ward neighbourhood in his 1951 article, "The Social System of a Slum":

> A noisy permissive atmosphere, bordering occasionally on licence, and simulating the freedom of the working man's living room is ... characteristic ... A fundamental norm is open acceptance of both idiosyncrasies of

The Head Brewer

The modern O'Keefe's Head Brewer is a highly trained specialist with six years of exacting training behind him as an apprentice and many years as an Assistant Head Brewer. Apprentices are specially selected from among brilliant university graduates. On joining O'Keefe's, they are issued with their apprentice badges of office — rubber boots and a rubber apron. Starting right at the bottom, they learn everything there is to know about brewing fine ale and beer, with an emphasis on the all-important quality control.

After serving six years' apprenticeship, they sit for examinations set by the British Institute of Brewing. Once past these exams, they can call themselves brewmasters, but they will continue their studies as Assistant Head Brewers in the O'Keefe's breweries.

Proof of the excellent training of O'Keefe's Head Brewers, is that six senior men hold the highest honour obtainable by a Brewer . . . Diploma Membership in the British Institute of Brewing.

6

Free Home Delivery

The well merited popularity of O'Keefe's Ale, Beer and Stout has necessitated a special order department wherever O'Keefe's Breweries are located.

Customers wishing O'Keefe's delivered to their homes, phone O'Keefe's Home Delivery, where a staff of polite and efficient telephone operators take your order and pass them on to the delivery department.

All Brewers' Retail Stores in Ontario carry your favourite O'Keefe's brew. Most will accept phone orders and make home deliveries.

7

ABOVE AND FACING PAGE: *Hate beer parlours? Home delivery via futuristic van was a phone call away.*

behaviour and moral outlook and different social types and races. Thus the handicapped, the man with no roof in his mouth, the half-breed, the negro, the wino and the transient, the prostitute, either pretty or emaciated, the homosexual, pimp or gambler are all accepted without stares or other forms of social ostracism.

To the beer parlour also goes the credit for making beer our national drink. Because they were for so long the main game in town, and beer the only beverage, anyone looking for a night out, however dreary, wound up drinking beer. During the Second World War, beer parlours introduced thousands of young men and women in uniform to the pleasures of public beer consumption, an experience they might never have had otherwise. (The contribution by Canadian brewers of beer to British NAAFI—Navy, Army and Air Force Institutes—canteens serving Canadian troops in Britain also played a role in boosting the number of Canadian beer drinkers.) Talk to anyone who attended university in the 1950s or 1960s, and you'll quickly learn that some unspeakable local beer parlour figures as much in their stories as memorable lectures or great teachers; maybe more. Horrible? Yes. But they were all we had.

5

THE RISE OF THE NATIONAL BRANDS

Frow the start of the twentieth century to its midpoint, there were no universal rules when it came to beer bottles. Ale bottles were green. Actually, *eastern* ale bottles were green. Western breweries tended to go with amber for both lager and ale. Another distinguishing feature was a bottle's shape. An eastern ale bottle—the one that held a pint, that is; quarts were a different matter—had a long neck leading into a gentle concave taper. Eastern lager bottles, however, had a short, narrow neck that bulged out quickly to form the base of the bottle. There was a lot of variation.

Now consider the stubby. A squat, brown, compact bottle, a no-necked fellow that looks as if it should be filled with liquid peroxide, not beer. Where's it from—east or west? And what's in it—ale or lager? Who knew? That ugly little bottle, a Canadian creation and the standard container for Canadian beer for the better part of a quarter century, beginning in 1962, could go anywhere and be filled with anything.

< *A Canadian soldier in Korea swigs Labatt's 1950 Anniversary Ale.*

Canadian beer bottles evolved from corked to capped to stubby.

When you look at that bottle—and then look back at the glorious regional, brewing, and company differences of earlier days—you see in a nutshell (or a nut-brown bottle) what happened to the Canadian beer industry and Canadian beer from the end of prohibition through the Second World War and almost to the 1980s. It's a story of consolidation and homogenization, of the rise of marketing and the shift of brewing from craft to large-scale industrial process, to the point where the people flogging it no longer referred to ale or lager, or even to beer, but simply to "liquid."

E.P. TAYLOR CAN claim at least some of the credit.

The man who later became famous as the owner of Kentucky Derby winner Northern Dancer was not what is sometimes called a "beer guy"—unlike John Molson, say. We don't even know if he drank beer, and he certainly brewed none personally.

Probably the best characterization of Taylor was "tycoon"—the kind of guy you see in old movies sitting at a desk dominated by six constantly ringing telephones. He dressed like a tycoon, too. Thanks to his long and successful connection with the sport of kings, Edward Plunket Taylor always seemed to be photographed in a top hat and cutaway coat, giving him the look of the little man on the Monopoly game. When most Canadians in the 1950s and 1960s thought of a millionaire, E.P. Taylor was who came to mind.

Born in Ottawa in 1901, Taylor got his start there working for his father selling bonds and securities, at which he proved a dab hand. His family also owned shares in Brading Brewery, a small Ottawa beer maker that survived prohibition by selling its ale in Quebec. Taylor was appointed to the Brading board in 1923, at the tender age of twenty-two.

When it began to look as though prohibition would end in Ontario, Taylor started to cogitate on the future prospects of the beer business there. Despite the impact of prohibition, Ontario was home to thirty-six competing breweries producing more than 150 brands. Apart from Labatt and to some extent

A dapper E.P. Taylor with his wife on their way to the races, 1960.

Carling, however, they were highly local outfits, often making do with old-fashioned equipment. None of them produced beer at anything like capacity. "I studied the whole brewing industry," Taylor later told his biographer, Richard Rohmer, "going back a hundred years in England and the United States, and I found the whole trend, as it was in any consumer business, was towards larger companies."

Actually, Taylor could figure out what was going to happen in Ontario just by looking at Quebec. In 1909, Montreal brewers Dawes & Co. and William Dow & Co. had consolidated their businesses with several other firms in the province. The new National Breweries took over such established Montreal names as Ekers' Brewery, G. Reinhardt & Sons, and the Montreal Brewing Company Ltd. Within a year, National had reduced its total number of breweries by half and ditched almost all of the brands it had bought, concentrating on Dawes (famed maker of Black Horse), Boswell, and Dow. The new behemoth dominated the Quebec market.

Brading gave E.P. Taylor his opening to change Canadian beer.

Moving to Toronto, where he worked for investment dealer McLeod Young Weir, Taylor spent what little spare time he had learning everything he could about Ontario's breweries. Identifying several likely takeover prospects, he approached the board of Brading.

Kicking off a major flurry of acquisitions in early 1930, just weeks after the Wall Street meltdown that triggered the Great Depression, might have struck many as less than optimal timing. But Taylor had already made moves to take over one brewery, the Kuntz plant in Waterloo, which was having financial problems.

Taylor didn't really have any money of his own (the Kuntz deal had been worked out by agreeing to swap Brading for Kuntz shares). By a happy coincidence, however, the owner of another brewery he was interested in purchasing put him in touch with someone who did—Clark

THE ORIGINAL KUNTZ BREWERY, WATERLOO.

Jennison, an Englishman who worked for a group of British investors. Taylor convinced Jennison that southern Ontario, with its growing population and reasonable transportation distances, was where real money could be made. A brand-new company, the Brewing Corporation of Ontario Limited, was born March 8, 1930.

Taylor's new company first took over the Taylor & Bate Brewery in St. Catharines. Next up was the British American Brewing Company in Windsor. In August, Taylor went after the Canadian Brewing Corporation Limited, a sort of brewing mini-conglomerate, which had breweries in Ontario and Manitoba.

Taylor planned one more acquisition for that year: Carling in London, Ontario. Successful at supplying the American bootleg market, the company had changed its name from the Carling Export Brewing and Malting Company to Carling Breweries in 1927, when prohibition ended in Ontario. It then began marketing a new beer in Ontario, Red Cap Ale. The label featured a

In the years before prohibition, Kuntz was Ontario's second-largest brewery.

83

NET CONTENTS 22 FLUID OUNCES
SERVE COLD

Niagara Spray BEER

CONTAINS LESS THAN 4.40% PROOF SPIRITS
EXPORT
CONTAINS MORE THAN 9% PROOF SPIRITS

ESTABLISHED 1834

TAYLOR & BATE ST CATHARINES — ONTARIO
LIMITED

Taylor & Bate supplied the Niagara region from 1834 until 1936, when it closed.

red-capped jockey—the idea of co-owner Harry Low, who, like E.P., was a horse racing fan.

Carling boasted a massive brewery and a bottling operation in Quebec as well, but the combined effect of the Canadian government's recent ban on beer exports to the United States (under pressure from President Herbert Hoover's administration) and the Depression had hurt the company. To stay afloat, Carling's owners borrowed money, using a lot of their shares as collateral. Taylor was able to make a deal with the bank, and at year's end of 1930 he held about 92 percent of Carling's shares. In a spree lasting not even a year, Taylor gained control of ten breweries. All told, the Brewing Corporation of Canada, as Taylor's company had been tellingly renamed in October of that year, accounted for 26 percent of the beer sold in Ontario, thirty-three separate brands in all.

What Taylor had done was incredibly risky. True, he hadn't put himself or his company deeply in debt, but he had placed his enterprise in a very exposed position. At this time, the belief was that for a brewery to be successful it needed to pump out 2.5 million gallons of beer a year—that's when economies of scale really started to kick in. Taylor had a few breweries that could turn out that, but none of the breweries he had bought, big or small, had been brewing at anything like capacity. To make matters worse, as the Depression deepened, beer consumption dropped, slipping from 6 gallons per capita in 1929 to a low of 3.5 in 1933.

There were no profits in 1930. Or the next year. Or indeed the year after that. Taylor's big break, which he himself largely engineered, was a change in the liquor laws in Ontario. Total prohibition was gone, but drinking was limited to home consumption. If only the province would allow the public sale of beer by the glass, it would boost business. With a provincial election coming in 1934, Taylor started working behind the scenes to make sure that whatever the outcome, he would be the winner. It worked. After Mitch Hepburn, the Liberal leader, won the election, his cabinet enacted an amendment to the Liquor Control Act that okayed the sale of beer by the glass. Anticipating the result, Taylor had made another grand acquisition—Toronto's O'Keefe's Brewing Company Ltd., on May 1, 1934. That same year, he also bought Cosgrove Export Brewery, another Toronto brewer. In 1935, for the first time, the Brewing Corporation of Canada finally showed a profit, albeit a slim $168,000.

After all these acquisitions, Taylor moved into high gear for the second phase of his plan—consolidation. Starting in 1936, Toronto's Dominion Brewing was shut down and its production shifted to the city's Cosgrove plant. That same year, many other plants in Ontario and Manitoba were sold or shut down. By 1938 the company, now renamed Canadian Breweries Limited, was running just six plants out of sixteen purchased and had reduced the number of brands it pumped out from more than fifty to twenty-seven. The streamlined company now controlled 30 percent of the

Dawes gave away these cards so that those on active service could order beer.

Consumer-friendly cardboard cases replaced wooden beer crates after the Second World War.

Ontario beer market, jumping to 34 percent the next year. Profits for 1938 were half a million dollars.

The outbreak of the Second World War would slow the changes, but Taylor had set the trend. Bigger would be better.

THE MOVE TOWARDS consolidation and homogenization that Taylor had set in motion in the 1930s really started picking up after the war. Following the deprivations of the war and the hard times of the 1930s, people had money to spend. One of the things they were spending it on was beer. In 1940, before wartime rationing came into effect, Canada's breweries produced three million barrels of beer; by 1950, they were pumping out seven million. Now that meant mostly bottled beer, not draft. More people were drinking beer at home. Refrigerators were becoming widespread, meaning you could keep it cold, and for the newly affluent veteran—and his wife and their friends—the nation's dingy beer parlours held no charms.

E.P. hadn't waited for the war to end before he'd got busy again, buying up more breweries. In 1944, with the end of hostilities in sight, he'd scooped up another three in Ontario: Capital, Bixel, and Walkerville. Now, in the postwar years, he got serious about making Canadian Breweries national in more than name. This, however, would not be easy. In 1928, as part of the everlasting see-saw between federal and provincial jurisdiction that has always defined the booze trade in this country (and pretty well everything else, with the possible exception of postage stamps), the feds had given the provinces the right to regulate their local alcohol trade. Most of them had slapped on tariffs or quotas that limited out-of-province beer or stopped it altogether. The biggest American breweries could sell pretty well everywhere across their nation, which led them to construct large breweries and concentrate the industry in relatively few cities. That could not happen in Canada.

To overcome this obstacle, Taylor started buying breweries nationwide. In 1953, he picked up Western Canada Breweries Limited, a holding company, which gave him Vancouver Breweries and Drewry's, which had breweries in Manitoba and Saskatchewan. He added another in Manitoba, Grant's, in 1954. In the east, he picked up the Frontenac Brewery in Quebec in 1951, and then he went after his long-ago inspiration, National Breweries. By the early

Cone-top cans could be filled on a bottling line, but were ultimately superseded by flat-top cans.

THE Stubby

Not just a stubby, a Molson Canadian stubby. It doesn't get any more iconic.

FOR MORE than two decades the stubby was the single-most distinctive feature of Canadian beer. As a piece of ingenious homegrown industrial design, it was as original in its day as today's Blackberry.

Well into the 1950s, Canadian brewers relied on a variety of different bottles for their beer. These traditional bottles tended to be very heavy, adding to transportation costs, and, thanks to their long necks, hard to store. As well, the green and clear versions of these bottles suffered from another drawback. Unlike amber glass, they did not protect the hops in beer from the damaging effects of ultra-violet rays, which can give beer a sulphurous "skunky" taste.

In 1958, the Brewers Association of Canada, which was made up of the big three and Canada's dozen or so surviving small brewers, decided to introduce a new universal bottle, which would be used by every brewery for every beer.

Known originally as the "compact" (*compacte* in French), this new amber bottle was a squat no-neck affair, an innovation that made it lighter but stronger than traditional bottles, and much easier to store in cartons. Rolled out for the press and brewery personnel in January 1961, the bottle was introduced for a six-month test in two selected markets—Peterborough, Ontario, and Rouyn, Quebec—on May 1, 1961.

Initially the bottle met with some skepticism, particularly from hotel waiters who claimed that it was far harder to open than traditional long-necked bottles. To remedy this, the bottle's original cone-shaped top was altered to the more familiar round shoulders of the classic stubby. At the end of the six-month test period, satisfied with what it had seen, the Brewers Association began preparing for the nationwide introduction of the stubby.

There was to be no phased or gradual introduction; instead, the switchover would happen all at once, on March 1, 1962. Three major glass companies (Dominion, Consumers, and Iroquois) were called in to produce the staggering first order of 288 million bottles (a quantity that, says noted beer bottle historian Patrick Hunter,

was equivalent to "12,000 truckloads of 2,000 bottles each"). These were distributed coast to coast in the few short months after the conclusion of the pilot program.

Whatever its aesthetic qualities (and some people complained that it looked like a medicine bottle), from the brewers' perspective, the stubby was a success—the bottle simplified shipping and transportation, and the short, tough stubby was good for numerous refills.

The stubby in many ways embodied all that was solid and stoic in the Canadian character. Think of the two adjectives most appropriately applied to it—"tough" and "squat"—and what it also brings to mind are the great goalies of that era, those stalwart unbreakable warriors who worked between the pipes: Johnny Bower, say, or even better, Gump Worsley. In another way, however, it symbolized the transformation of the Canadian beer industry. The rapid and universal adoption of the stubby was possible only because of concentration in the hands of three big players that also controlled retailing in their biggest market, Ontario. What mattered was getting the fluid out there, cheaply and efficiently. From consumers' point of view, like it or not, the stubby was what we were going to get.

The generic labels on these stubbies reveal what was happening to Canadian beer.

89

CARLING'S *Famous Beer*

NOW PRODUCED IN **DREWRYS** NEW $1,000,000 ADDITION

The Carling Breweria (Manitoba) Limited

ABOVE: *Buying regional powerhouse Drewry's let Taylor dominate Manitoba and Saskatchewan.*

BELOW: *Taylor gained a toehold in Quebec by purchasing Montreal's Frontenac in 1951.*

1950s, National was in trouble. The original managers hadn't concentrated on cultivating their successors, and there were quality problems as well. In 1951, the brewery suffered ruined batches, a problem typically caused by rogue bacteria. This had hit Black Horse particularly hard and led, at one point, to all of National's Montreal brands being withdrawn from the market. Taylor made a merger offer to Norman Dawes, the head of National. When that was rebuffed, Canadian Breweries started buying up National shares, garnering about 47 percent of the total. It wasn't enough for control but at the next shareholders' meeting, in March 1952, Taylor managed to get his slate elected, rather than the group nominated by National's management. The move gave him effective control of the company.

Taylor now controlled breweries stretching from Quebec to the Pacific. As happened in Ontario, anywhere there was duplication, breweries were shut down or sold off, and the survivors were left brewing a small number of brands—mainly O'Keefe, Carling, and Brading. To take advantage of its popularity in Quebec, Taylor added Dow to this select group of brands after he took over National.

AS A CONSOLIDATOR, Taylor was first out of the gates, but he soon had competition on the national scene. By the end of the war, Molson and Labatt had both transformed themselves from privately held family firms into publicly traded companies. Now able to raise substantial amounts of capital through stock issues, they were looking at expanding. To an extent, they would follow Taylor's path by buying smaller breweries, though there were fewer around by this point. If need be, they would build anew.

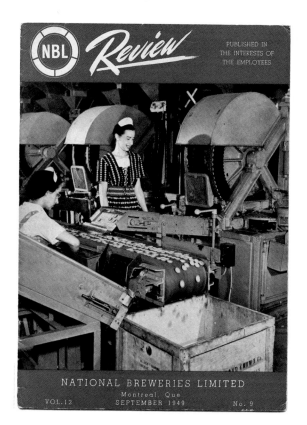

NBL *Review*

PUBLISHED IN
THE INTERESTS OF
THE EMPLOYEES

NATIONAL BREWERIES LIMITED
Montreal, Que.
VOL. 12   SEPTEMBER 1949   No. 9

They didn't stray far from home at first: London's Labatt moved into Quebec and Manitoba, while Montreal's Molson extended into Ontario. They may have been tentative because historically such a move into new provinces would mean confronting Canada's differing regional beer tastes. Luckily for them, consumer taste was helping to solve that challenge. The nationwide trend to milder-tasting beers, one that had started back in the late nineteenth century and had accelerated after the First World War, meant that people actively sought less original brews. Separate beers grew less distinct, lagers and ales grew closer together. Both Molson and Labatt modified two of their mainstays, Export and IPA, respectively.

They both also introduced new brands, which for the first time were based on recipes that made heavy use of adjuncts like corn in the brewing process—giving the beer a slightly sweet and very mild flavour. Labatt was first off the mark, producing its new Fiftieth Anniversary Ale in 1950 to commemorate the anniversary of John and Hugh Labatt joining the company. Next, the company introduced a new lager, known simply as Pilsener, which was created after a visit by Hugh to Czechoslovakia in 1950. To create a uniform

With multiple plants and revered brands, National truly was Quebec's brewer.

91

Anniversary Ale (above) and Pilsener (right) were Labatt's bids to gain new customers.

identity, the two new brands, along with pre-existing IPA and Crystal Lager, were given snappy modern labels featuring swirly concentric circles, but colour-coded: red for IPA, yellow for Crystal, green for Fiftieth Anniversary Ale, and blue for Pilsener. In the way of these things, Anniversary Ale quickly became redubbed 50—"Fifty" or, in Quebec, *"Cinquante."* The new Pilsener would morph into Blue.

Molson also introduced new brews in the early 1950s—an ale, known as Molson Golden, and that same year, 1954, the company's first-ever lager in its almost 170 years of brewing history: Crown and Anchor. Brewed at the company's new plant on the Toronto waterfront, Crown and Anchor would be renamed in 1959—as Canadian, the most iconic beer name imaginable in this country (at least outside Quebec, where it was never marketed). It was a

signal that the big brewers were now aspiring to place their products from sea to shining sea.

From a flavour perspective, these new beers—brewed from market-driven recipes and plumped with mellow-making adjuncts—could only be described as innocuous. If there was nothing, really, that attracted drinkers, there was nothing that would turn them off either. There was little to separate what Labatt made from what Molson or Canadian Breweries turned out.

Canadian brewing had been transformed, as if stricken with gigantism. In 1945, even after E.P. Taylor's buying sprees, Canada still had thirty-one separate brewing companies running sixty-one plants. By the early 1960s, by contrast, ten companies ran fifty-one breweries. Twenty-five of those were in the hands of Molson, Labatt, and Canadian Breweries. Needless to say, they dominated the market by volume, together accounting for almost 94 percent of the beer sold in Canada. (Canadian Breweries had a 47 percent share, Molson 27, and Labatt a little under 20.) From coast to coast, venerable local breweries bit the dust through the fifties and into the sixties: Prairie powerhouse Sicks' was swallowed by Molson in 1958; Labatt had

LEFT: *Before it morphed into Blue, Labatt's Pilsener featured a tiny, cuddly Bavarian.*

RIGHT: *Fifty boasted its own mascot, "Monsieur Cinquante," a stylized lumberjack.*

B.C.'s Lucky Lager fell prey to Labatt's national dreams in 1958.

grabbed Shea's in Manitoba in 1953 and got Lucky in B.C. in 1958. Canadian Breweries took over Edmonton's Bohemian Maid in 1961. Newfoundland lost all three of its independent breweries in one year, 1962, with the big three grabbing one apiece. By the early 1960s, only Nova Scotia and New Brunswick, where separate branches of the estimable Oland family controlled each province's respective top brewery, remained outside the behemoths' embrace.

Local protests, if any, were muted. Maybe the bitter aftertaste of prohibition, with its general disapproval of alcohol, made loyal customers reluctant to speak out against the loss of their favourite firms. The big guys kept a few local brands for old times' sake—Labatt's kept Lucky in B.C., Molson kept Old Style Pilsner across the west—but otherwise a tsunami of pale beer swept over the country.

Nor did the government seem overly concerned with the concentration of so major an industry in so few hands. (In fact the Co-operative Commonwealth Federation, forerunner to the New Democratic Party, characteristically suggested that the industry be nationalized—concentrated, in other words, in a single pair of hands that also regulated the flow. A government-owned brewer—back in the days when most nationalized Canadian enterprises were about as customer-friendly as a Soviet ball-bearing plant—was perhaps the only thing that could have made the big three seem warm and cuddly.)

The government did make some feeble efforts to reverse the trend towards industry concentration. In February 1954, it announced it was investigating E.P. Taylor and Canadian Breweries for possible violations of the Combines

Investigation Act, going back to the takeover of National Breweries a few years before. The case dragged on for several years, and was finally heard in 1959. It was then neatly dismissed, the presiding judge finding that Taylor and company had not restricted trade in any way by buying up so many companies. Prices were set by the provincial governments, operating, it must be assumed, in the interests of the general public. Basically, it was a green light for all of them to keep on buying breweries.

Seemed the big three were in the catbird seat.

They were titans—but history has shown that it's not always clear sailing for the titanic. The stubby of triumph they grasped was a poisoned chalice.

In scarcely more than a generation, they would all be gone—victims of a global gigantism that dwarfed their own ambitions.

LEFT: *Beer cans appeared only briefly postwar, but took off in the 1960s.*

RIGHT: *The old "quart" bottle—really 22 ounces—outlived the stubby.*

6

MOBILE BILLBOARDS AND YODELLING COWBOYS

E.P. TAYLOR played a part in bringing into existence that brown bottle and all it stood for, to be sure. But it wasn't just him. In the 1930s, at the same time as Taylor was starting to build his empire, the world of consumer products (and that includes beer) was changing. For the first time, companies were starting to think about the very idea of a "consumer," as opposed to a plain old-fashioned customer who bought something. And the something was turning into a "consumer product."

This was a startling notion for Canadian brewers. Up to then, the top man in the firm after the owner had been the brewmaster. Addressed always with the prefix "Mr.," brewmasters had often served lengthy apprentice-ships or attended a brewing school, and were true old-world craftsmen. The best ones stayed with their breweries for decades. John Hyde, who became Molson's brewmaster in 1879, held the job until 1930, when he was suc-ceeded by his son, William, who remained with the company until the 1950s.

< *Workers on the bottling line at Molson in the 1930s.*

The beer business had revolved around these men—they went off and made beer, they made it to their liking, and when they said it was ready, the company could go about selling it. There wasn't really any of what we would today call sophisticated marketing. The general approach was summed up in a line attributed to John Molson: "An honest brew makes its own friends."

This attitude started to change in the 1930s. Whether driven by the need to survive hard economic times or a new understanding of the power of surveys and statistics, all manner of companies, not just brewers, started trying to find out what made their customers tick—or drink, as the case may be.

For the breweries, this new approach became particularly pertinent as the Depression worsened and beer sales dropped. What would become Canada's three dominant beer companies in the postwar period—Labatt, Molson, and Canadian Breweries—all latched onto consumer surveys.

Presumably one of the first areas to be probed was the flavour of brewers' offerings. To this day, every company in the food and drink business relies on extensive, often blind, tastings to tweak their products.

Executives at Sicks' Breweries (one wearing spats) discuss a marketing campaign.

So what exactly did they learn? And how did they respond? We are entering a fraught area. Brewers are loath to reveal their recipes, and pretty reticent about ever admitting that their beers change over time. After all, "old-fashioned value" and "unchanging quality" are powerful selling tools in a business that runs so much on people's perceptions. Indeed, one of the brewmaster's traditional jobs was to make sure that the beer *didn't* change.

Although the findings of those early consumer surveys were closely guarded, other evidence tells us that in fact tastes were changing. The beer makers were now selling to the first generation of Canadians raised on soft drinks. They were also selling more to women, who weren't as fond of the strong, full-bodied ales that had dominated the brewers' offerings to that point (a taste they still haven't acquired, recent surveys in the United Kingdom suggest). In addition, as beer expert Stephen Beaumont explained to me, during prohibition "people slaked their not inconsiderable thirsts with bad liquor mixed with sweet sodas, thus creating a social palate more comfortable with sweetness than bitterness."

Whatever the cause, and it was probably some mixture of all three factors, the brewers began modifying their recipes to meet shifting tastes. Molson had already played around with its beers at the turn of the twentieth century; now it did it again. How? In his book on the Molsons, *The Barley and the Stream,* the otherwise dependable Merrill Denison grows a little coy on this point, slipping into the passive voice: "New formulae were suggested, and various changes were made in processing," he says, changes involving "the selection of malt and hops, the temperatures for sparging and boiling, and so forth." (*Ah, yes,* you think, *the sparging. That explains it.* Then you wonder: *What the hell is sparging?* In fact, sparging is a complicated process of adding water to the mash in the early stages of brewing. It is doubtful that changing the temperature would make any great difference to flavour.)

What this probably came down to was reducing the amount of malt used in the brewing, lowering the alcohol content, and probably

Would a beer named Sicks' be launched today?

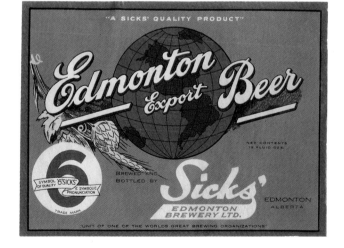

switching from darker to lighter roasted malts, which would reduce the "beer-iness" of the brew's flavour. Having cut down on the sweet malt, a reduction in bitter hops would also make sense. What's left is essentially beer with some of the edges knocked off.

Molson seems to have been the leader in this, but Labatt's surveys were telling them the same things. They modified their famed India Pale Ale a few years later, making it less hoppy and hence less bitter, or—as the brewers like to say—rendering it "lighter" tasting. Probably Canadian Breweries was at it as well—in his history of the company, *Vision in Action,* Albert A. Shea reports they had similar surveys carried out. Shutting down brands and shifting production, as the company did through the 1930s, would have provided a good opportunity to change recipes—especially as, in many cases, they would be selling the surviving brands in areas where they had never been well known.

The brewmaster had been dethroned. In his place, the salesman would now rule. In an even more significant change, voices from outside—the ad

men and their survey wizards—would counsel those who led the brewing empires.

It's not that the brewers had ignored the sales side of the business in the past. But their methods, forged both by tradition and government restrictions on what they could do, were simple. In the late nineteenth century, for example, Labatt depended on just two "travellers," as they were called, one of whom ranged as far west as Portage la Prairie, Manitoba—and this was before the Canadian Pacific Railway had been finished. Molson relied on but a single salesman, H.E. Halde, to promote their products in Quebec outside Montreal. Something of a legend, Halde departed Montreal every Monday by horse and buggy. Every town he visited boasted at least two hotels, often more, and in the interests of selling Molson's products he was obliged to eat and drink at all of them. Friday would see him returning to the city, orders in hand and the springs of his carriage straining under his ever-expanding bulk.

Beer companies had also advertised before, largely through newspaper ads and giveaways (and they were still using the latter technique—Labatt, for

An early attempt by Calgary Brewing to "harness" the power of their brand.

Two salesmen from Quebec's National Breweries take orders from a club owner.

instance, handed out 100,000 complimentary ashtrays of varying designs in the 1930s). But they hadn't been very systematic about it. In 1898, no one at a brewery sat down and said, "We're targeting the younger, more affluent Klondike prospector, the sourdough who doesn't mind spending his precious gold nuggets for a quality product."

Even if they had wanted to, they couldn't have. In most parts of Canada, thanks to the same puritanical mindset that had brought in prohibition and then Canada's joy-defying beer parlours, liquor advertising was either severely limited or banned outright. (This isn't ancient history, either: Saskatchewan lifted their provincial ban only in 1987; until 1997 in PEI, you couldn't even have the name of a brewery on the side of a delivery truck.) Given how little actual selling the brewers' agents could do, it's appropriate that they were known as travellers rather than salesmen.

It was the need to start carrying out consumer surveys that, in a roundabout way, changed all of that. The brewers lacked the specialized skills that consumer surveys demand. So, for the first time, they turned to advertising agencies, which were pioneering this new science (or pseudo-science, as some would argue). Doing so brought about a profound change in their advertising practices as well. Molson turned to Cockfield Brown, the leader in market research at the time. Labatt went with the Toronto office of the American giant J. Walter Thompson. Canadian Breweries picked Toronto's McKim Advertising, founded in 1889 and Canada's oldest ad agency.

Inside the companies, the sales manager became a key figure, and the brewers started looking for high-quality people for the job. When Canadian Breweries decided they needed a proper sales manager, for example, they hired away the man from McKim who had done their market surveys, J. Smith-Ross. The breweries' sales staffs ballooned with new travellers, a throng of glad-handing extroverts with cast-iron livers and nicknames like "Doc." These hale fellows each concentrated on getting their firm's beer into hotel beverage rooms, the one real point of human contact the brewers had with their customers. Travellers were the companies' conduits to their customers. The smart companies knew to listen to them.

In the end, though, it was the ad agencies—and the top-notch inside sales staff the brewers hired to act on their advice—that helped overcome the government restrictions on advertising that stood in the way of the breweries' growth.

Quebec, always more liberal than the rest of the country, had already provided a hint of what was to come. The 1920s had seen the province's breweries embroiled in a billboard war. Upstart Frontenac Breweries, founded in 1914, kicked off the struggle with the offer of cash prizes. On opening a bottle, drinkers could check the underside of the cap and see if they had won anywhere from one to five dollars. As customers were lured away by this gimmick, National and Molson cut their prices in retaliation. The whole situation quickly escalated into a three-way, province-wide outdoor advertising campaign.

Frontenac's assault featured immense billboards—60 feet across by 20 feet high—scattered across the countryside. National struck back

Now gone, Black Horse Ale once boasted a cult-like following.

In the 1920s, Dawes Black Horse dominated the Quebec landscape.

with immense wooden silhouettes of the trademark Percheron horse featured on the Dawes Black Horse bottle. Zagging where the others had zigged, Molson came up with the simple yet effective idea of painting barns red and then emblazoning them with the words *La Bière Molson*.

Ultimately, perhaps worried about either the aesthetic effect of their ever-escalating advertising war or its growing cost, the Quebec Brewers Association suggested to the provincial government that it might want to pass legislation outlawing billboards before every available farmer's field from the Gatineau Hills to the Gaspé was festooned with outsized brewery ads. Even in La Belle Province, there were limits. National would later develop an ingenious scheme that didn't violate the law's letter, but sure played with its spirit: they offered farmers in Quebec the use of handsome black Percherons, for stud, free of charge, or for sale as draft animals at a very good price. Whether ploughing or grazing in a farmer's field, the horses acted as living billboards for the brewery's flagship brand. Think of it as the first viral advertising campaign.

IN ONTARIO, IT fell largely to one remarkable man, Hugh MacKenzie, to navigate deftly through the thicket of rules and regulations that hampered beer marketing in Canada. In the process, he helped set the tone for most Canadian beer advertising to this day.

ABOVE: *Second-order marketing— a coaster highlighting not a beer, but an ad campaign.*

Educated at the Royal Military College in Kingston and trained as an accountant before he joined Labatt as comptroller (later becoming sales manager), MacKenzie deserves exclusive credit for one of the most ingenious advertising gambits in the history of the Canadian beer business.

Ontario's restrictions on beer advertising at this point could best be explained in terms of what you couldn't do. Print ads were taboo (though after 1936 what might be called "general service" ads, ones that could get the name out but say nothing about the product, were okay). Anything like an in-store promotion was a no-no. The Brewers Warehousing stores that had been

BELOW: *Famed Canadian sculptor Ross Butler created Black Horse statues for Dawes.*

105

set up to sell beer were by regulation scrupulously neutral—there could be no ads favouring any one brewer, and the product was hidden well away. Nor did the regulations allow for any sort of outdoor advertising like neon signs or billboards.

MacKenzie's wife had suggested the company create some sort of "mobile billboard." While thumbing through an issue of *Esquire,* he found just the man to deliver it—Count Alexis de Sakhnoffsky, a Russian-born industrial designer who had developed streamlined cars in Europe for Vanden Plas and in the United States for Auburn, Nash, and others. In his role as the new magazine's "technical editor," each month he turned out pages of drawings of futuristic cars and airplanes.

MacKenzie hired Sakhnoffsky in 1935 to develop a fantastic teardrop-shaped semi-truck for Labatt. By 1939, eighteen of the bright red streamliners were breezing along Ontario's highways, their sides emblazoned in gold with the single word "Labatt's" in a script based on the signature of the second John Labatt. Dressed in tailored uniforms, tested on their mechanical knowledge, and trained in first aid, Labatt's drivers had strict orders: wherever they

Flash Gordon would not have looked out of place at the wheel of a Labatt truck.

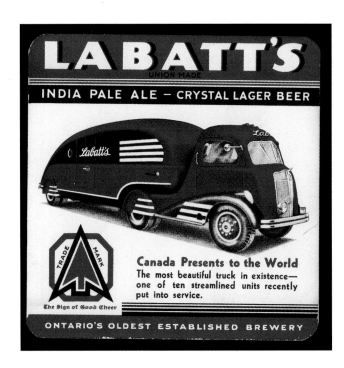

THE BIRTH OF THE
Lifestyle Ad

AFTER the day's work—
a bottle of O'Keefe's
"Pilsener" Lager.

When you come home all tired
out, a bottle of O'Keefe's "Pilsener"
will take the tiredness all away.

O'Keefe's "Pilsener" Lager is
concentrated strength, vigor and
refreshment. As a food-tonic—as
a strength-giver and reviver—
nothing surpasses this delicious,
sparkling lager.

Keep it in the house—enjoy a
bottle after a hard day's work.

Order a case from your dealer.

O'Keefe's
PILSENER LAGER

"The Light Beer In The
Light Bottle."

292

*Traditional beer
ads were as close as
advertising got to
mumbling.*

HUGH MACKENZIE cracked the door on advertising beer in most of Canada; Mark Napier kicked it wide open, giving us the ads we still see today.

Most of the beer ads in Canadian magazines of the 1930s were straightforward affairs: a picture of the bottle, maybe a simple line illustration, and a brief slug of type. Napier's ads were different. He had researched Labatt's history and used what he'd learned to tell its story. Carried in upscale magazines like *Mayfair* and *Canadian Homes and Gardens*, Labatt ads typically boasted a half-page colour illustration. One featured an attractive couple on a cottage dock engaged in earnest conversation with an older gentleman. Another showed two men at a hunting lodge. In a third, a crusty old salt complete with captain's hat and parrot dispensed wisdom to a firm-jawed, business-suited gentleman. But while the scene and the characters changed, the topic was always the same: the timeless qualities of Labatt's India Pale Ale. "It's not an accident it tastes so good today," one ad kicked off. "Taste it," our ancient mariner exhorted his skeptical listener, "and you'll see." Albert Tucker's unpublished history of Labatt quotes Napier's own take on their strategy: "We didn't *sell* beer. We just told a picturesque historical story . . ."

One of the most interesting qualities of Napier's ads was what might be called their aspirations. Beer might still be a largely working-class drink, but there was nothing working class about the magazines the Labatt ads appeared in, or the people and the scenes featured in them. Beer was getting ambitions to climb the social ladder.

His ads were, we would say now, selling a lifestyle. They were also making a virtue out of a necessity. Faced with a thicket of regulation, and obliged to be mindful not to offend the sensibilities of Canada's temperance forces (still feared by politicians and brewers alike, neither of whom had any desire to stomp on that particular hornet's nest), Napier developed a unique approach to advertising and marketing beer: hard sell was a no-no; the approach would be oblique, the ad sidling up to its topic crab-style, as allusive as good poetry. There's an old saying that in advertising you sell the sizzle, not the steak. Following Napier's path, Canadian beer advertising would not only focus on the sizzle, but for a long time the steak wouldn't even be in the picture.

Labatt's ads, by contrast, literally sang to the customer.

Top Quebec comedian Arthur Lefebvre sings the praises of IPA in a testimonial ad.

saw a car in trouble, they were to pull over immediately and offer assistance. As advertising, the trucks were entirely permissible and absolutely unforgettable. As marketers, their drivers generated enormous goodwill.

Hugh MacKenzie didn't stop there. One day in 1936, MacKenzie walked into the offices of the J. Walter Thompson advertising agency in Toronto, and introduced himself by saying, "My company is not allowed to advertise. Will you take the account?" Perhaps warming to a challenge, J. Walter Thompson's executives agreed and assigned an Englishman named Mark Napier to work on Labatt.

Ontario prohibited liquor and beer advertising, but there were ways around the ban. No province restricted magazines that came in from other parts of the country. In the 1930s, Montreal was home to many English-language magazines that had the bulk of their circulation outside the province. Labatt began to use these to hit the audience they wanted to sell to in Ontario. (In 1940, E.P. Taylor went them one better and actually founded his own magazine, entitled *New World*. Ostensibly based in Montreal, it was in fact put together in Toronto—Morley Callaghan was a regular contributor—and its specific purpose was to circumvent Ontario's ban on beer ads.)

Although highly regulated, the exciting new medium of radio also gave brewers a way to reach drinkers. In Quebec, beer companies were prohibited from buying ads on the radio, but paradoxically they could sponsor shows. At 7:45 PM, beginning on October 1, 1932, Montreal audiences could tune in to hear Virginia Fair greet them on local radio with "Good evening, everybody, this is the Dow Girl." Starting in 1936, Labatt paid for regular newscasts on Montreal radio station CKAC, along with a brief drama based on a delivery boy character they had developed to use in their newspaper ads there. In 1938, they took on a French-language show called *Les Amours de Ti-Jos*, a mixture of comedy and music based on the weekly adventures of a young grocer's apprentice. The show was broadcast in four cities across Quebec. To hit southern Ontario, Labatt sponsored a show broadcast from Buffalo, New York, called *International House Party*. This variety show hit radio audiences in Labatt's traditional stronghold, where the company was otherwise forbidden from using the airwaves.

Other breweries used radio, too. In the early 1940s, again taking advantage of Quebec's more relaxed laws, Canadian Breweries backed *Radio Carabin*, a French-language variety show. Sponsored first by their O'Keefe brands and then by Brading, the popular show cost Taylor's company nearly $100,000 a year to underwrite.

Listeners in southern Ontario were the target of a particularly crafty bit of advertising. Each week they could tune into Hamilton's CKOC to enjoy a homegrown show that just happened to bear the name *The Black Horse Tavern*. Not, of course, that the

Conscious of a potential market, Labatt also advertised in French in Quebec.

● Demandez à votre épicier! Demandez-lui pourquoi! Il vous dira, "Le goût! Et c'est vrai! Mais comme il est très occupé il n'aura pas le temps de vous expliquer pourquoi la Labatt possède cette saveur moelleuse, piquante et différente que de plus en plus de gens préfèrent. En voici donc la raison: L'India Pale Ale Labatt est encore brassée d'après la formule originale que John Labatt le second apprit d'un brasseur anglais en 1862. Elle est brassée avec de l'eau de puits profonde de London, Canada. Elle est longuement et patiemment vieillie. Et quand vous vous régalez de Labatt, remarquez comme, sa saveur s'attarde agréablement sur le palais après que la bière est toute bue.

"take five" for fifty ale*

"EXCITEMENT HIGH?" Then take time out for a brew-break. But make the most of it . . . make the "L" sign for light, likable Labatt's 50 Ale . . . brewed with just the *heart* of the hops for a perfect balance of vigour and smoothness. Buy a case tomorrow and see why Labatt's 50 is Canada's fastest growing ale.

50

WATCH CANADIAN PRO FOOTBALL
on the CTV network, brought to you by Labatt's. See TV page for station.

★6339 — Newspapers—5 cols. x 200 lines — October issues.

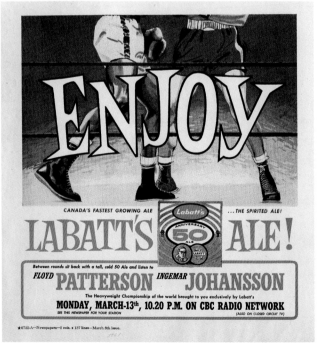

ENJOY

CANADA'S FASTEST GROWING ALE   . . .THE SPIRITED ALE!

LABATT'S **50** **ALE!**

Between rounds sit back with a tall, cold 50 Ale and listen to

FLOYD **PATTERSON** INGEMAR **JOHANSSON**

The Heavyweight Championship of the world brought to you exclusively by Labatt's

MONDAY, MARCH-13th, 10.20 P.M. ON CBC RADIO NETWORK
SEE THIS NEWSPAPER FOR YOUR STATION   (ALSO ON CLOSED CIRCUIT TV)

★6722-A—Newspapers—5 cols. x 137 lines—March 9th issue.

beer was in any way connected with the program—as noted above, in Ontario mentions of beer and breweries were entirely banned from the airwaves. Skeptics would have noticed, however, that photographs of the show's cast in fancy dress did feature the tavern's distinctive equine symbol, which bore a strong resemblance to that of a well-known Quebec ale.

LIKE SO MUCH connected with Canadian beer, advertising altered after the end of the Second World War. Banned for the duration of the war, the traditional forms of advertising were laid to rest for good in Ontario (the biggest market, and home to two of the three nascent national brewers) in 1946, when the government banned point-of-purchase advertising as part of a move to clean up the beverage rooms. That pretty well wiped out the old-style giveaway beer tray and other traditional promotional items. No, now the brewers had to reach out through national magazines like *Maclean's* or *Saturday Night* or, even more importantly, the new medium of television, which was just hitting Canada at the same time as the new national brands were being launched. This being Canada, it barely needs saying that federal regulators initially banned alcohol commercials from radio and television. These regulations were not relaxed until 1955.

Canadian brewers had developed their allusive advertising style in the 1930s, but the regulations they had to deal with to advertise on television tried even their skills—no one was to be shown drinking; originally no bottles or glasses were to be shown either; the ad could, however, feature a disembodied label at the end, so long as it was entirely separate from the action of the preceding commercial. The ad agencies rose to the challenge. Early Canadian beer ads achieved an almost Zen-like emptiness, the celebration of a product that was to be found everywhere except within the confines of the commercial itself. You might find yourself watching a group of adenoidal cowboys gathered around a campfire yodelling the word "Fifty" repeatedly, or a bearded professor demonstrating how the rhythm inherent in the O'Keefe "V-I-E-N-N-A" singing commercial might create countless untoward results, not least among them the purchase of beer. But people actually drinking beer? Nah. In a weird way, though, the ads made sense. A commercial spot featuring real Canadians drinking in a real Canadian beer parlour would have been too depressing to watch—who would have written it, Samuel Beckett? The ads did their job—they got the name out there.

And they did more than that. It's hard to believe today, but in the 1950s and early 1960s, beer ads were virtually the only popular culture Canadians had, except for Don Messer, Howard the Turtle, and the Plouffe family. Beer ads were one thing we all had in common. Even if you didn't drink beer, you knew the ads and the catchphrases—"Wouldn't a Dow Go Good Now?" Or "Take Five for Fifty Ale." It seemed fitting somehow. If beer was our national drink, and the beer parlour our national watering hole, then why shouldn't the beer commercial be our national art form?

ABOVE AND FACING PAGE: *Connecting beer with sports helped brewers reach a receptive audience.*

7

BEERADAMMERUNG! TWILIGHT OF THE TITANS

STARTING IN the 1960s and picking up speed in the 1970s and 1980s, Canada began at long last to shake off the hangover of the prohibition era. Perhaps it was the influx of European immigrants after the war. Or part of the sixties' distrust of authority and skepticism about outdated social mores. Or just a growing national sophistication. Whatever the reason, beer drinking, drinking in general, in this country changed. Old windows were opened up. You could get something to eat besides pickled eggs. Pretty young waitresses replaced the guy with the metal tray, the comb-over, and the change maker on his belt. Bars opened on Sunday. You could drink in them standing up, at an *actual* bar, and you could pick up a beer and walk ten feet with it. You could even drink on a patio outside. If you were a man, you could enter a room in a bar where women were drinking and not be shown the door. If you were a woman, you could enter on your own and not be watched suspiciously by the bar staff for improper conduct.

< *Newly legal eighteen-year-old drinkers in Toronto, 1971.*

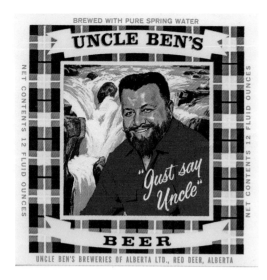

TOP: *"Uncle" Ben Ginter tried creating a new national brewery in the 1970s, and failed.*

ABOVE: *In the 1960s and '70s the big three moved from sponsoring sports to owning teams.*

Simple facts, but unthinkable to Canadians even a few short years before. The brewers were thriving too. From the introduction of the national brands in the 1950s, Molson, Labatt, and Canadian Breweries had just kept expanding. Along the way Canadian Breweries morphed into Carling O'Keefe, after being acquired by international cigarette giant Rothmans of Pall Mall. E.P. Taylor, who had long used his earnings from Canadian Breweries to underwrite his other business deals, walked away with a handsome chunk of change from his interest.

Sometimes it seemed as if the biggest challenge facing the brewers was figuring out what to do with the money they made. They acquired other businesses of all types: food, dairy, chocolate, and furniture, to name a few. All three poured money into sports, too. Molson had a decades-long on-again, off-again relationship with the Montreal Canadiens (selling the team in 1971, then buying it back in the late seventies); Labatt had brought major league baseball to Toronto (and created a TV network, TSN, dedicated to pro sports); Carling O'Keefe owned the Toronto Argonauts and the Quebec Nordiques.

By the beginning of the 1980s, the big three Canadian breweries held 96 percent of the beer market. Of the forty beer plants in Canada, they owned thirty-two. They were in competition with each other, yes, but well protected behind a thicket of federal and provincial regulations that shielded them from price wars, foreign interlopers, and the danger of domestic upstarts. In Ontario, the largest market, the three of them jointly owned the Brewers Retail (formerly called Brewers Warehousing) stores, the major distribution channel for all the beer sold in the province. In hockey terms, they were like a team whose opponent had unaccountably failed to show up: their sole challenge was to see how fast they could flick pucks into an empty net.

Then it would all unravel.

ONE OF THE most profound changes in Canadian beer-drinking culture occurred in the early 1970s. Across the country, governments cut the drinking age, generally from twenty-one to eighteen (though a few provinces later raised it to nineteen)—just as what might be called the crest of the baby boom of the 1950s were entering their late teens and early twenties.

Their overwhelming numbers made it a youth-besotted era, and beer companies scrambled to jump onto the bandwagon. Previous generations of beer drinkers had been largely happy to drink what their elders drank; now, a stigma started to develop around what business journalist Paul Brent termed "Dad's beer" in his book *Lager Heads*. They cared about their beer—you were, to some extent, what you drank. Brewers wanted these kids. The time was ripe: not only were there a lot of them, but also they were at the age when drinking a lot of beer was central to their existence. Their loyalties weren't fixed yet, either, which was even more attractive. Hook 'em young, the theory went, and they were yours for life.

What was in the bottle was almost irrelevant—at least that was the beer companies' attitude. It was all about perceptions, and that led right to marketing. As if in anticipation, beer advertising had started changing even before the drinking age was lowered. Long-time Toronto advertising executive Douglas Linton characterizes 1950s beer ads as being "guys in flannel shirts comparing trout flies." They were aiming at an older audience, and, says Linton, anyone advertising alcohol had to keep an eye out: "Don't go too young, don't go too sexy, because you might get in trouble with the regulatory people."

With time, however, the regulations began to relax. On TV, Molson Golden's ads led the way in the mid-1960s, but the Labatt campaigns that started in 1968 and ran in various manifestations for over a decade probably marked the true revolution. They were created by the Toronto office of J. Walter Thompson.

Until the 1960s, beer was very much a male, blue-collar beverage.

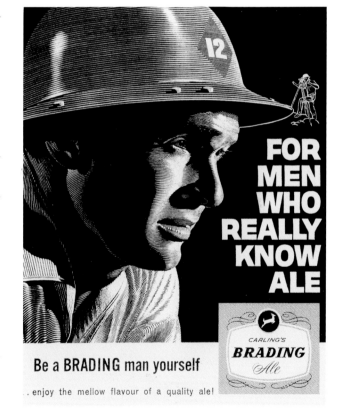

FOR MEN WHO REALLY KNOW ALE

Be a BRADING man yourself

CARLING'S
BRADING
Ale

. . enjoy the mellow flavour of a quality ale!

The brainchild of the agency's Bob Byron, the Labatt's Blue commercials went through almost countless variations over the years. They were frequently set in a Canada of eternal summer. They typically featured some activity (grass skiing, scuba diving, even table hockey) and included lots of cheery shots of attractive people. The music was a variant of the old song "When You're Smiling," and at the commercial's finale, a trademark bright-blue hot-air balloon would float across a cloudless azure sky as somewhere a celestial jingle choir sang, "Blue, Blue, Blue, Blue, Blue, Blue Labatt's Blue."

The new Blue look lifted the allusive and aspirational qualities of Canadian beer advertising to previously unscaled heights. Forget hard sell or soft sell. They didn't sell beer at all. They hawked abstract nouns like "freedom" and "happiness," which the perceptive viewer could, in fact, combine into the concrete thought: "free to get happy on many beers." The early Blue ads set the tone for every beer ad to come, right up to arguably the greatest beer commercial ever created, the famed Molson "Rant."

SOMEONE BACK IN the 1960s gifted with foresight could probably have predicted many of the changes in drinking habits and the beer business that came about in the 1970s and 1980s. But there was one shift that no one who knew Canada and Canadian beer would likely have seen coming. Historically,

Canadians had disdained American beer. The more polite among us would have commented that it was watery. Blunter drinkers would have likened it to urine—human, horse, or otherwise. That was a sentiment many Americans shared, often preferring to buy such popular imports to the U.S. as Molson Golden.

Our beer was better, stronger, and tastier. At least, that was what we told ourselves. And, once upon a time, it might have been true. In practice, however, Canada's beer culture had been converging with American beer tastes for going on a century. Western Canadian brewing was strongly influenced by German/American traditions. In most parts of Canada, lager had bumped ale as our favourite kind of beer. The most popular lager through most of the seventies was Blue, a pilsner brewed using such adjuncts as corn, just like its American cousins. Moreover, American beers weren't, in the main, much weaker than Canadian ones. Reality was all very well, but Canadians held on to this particular set of beliefs.

Then in June 1980, Labatt struck a deal with Anheuser-Busch to brew Budweiser in Canada. The company announced that Canadian Budweiser would be five percent alcohol by volume (the American version was in fact generally the same strength). The initial ads also included a close-up of the label showing the exact Canadian alcohol content.

When push came to shove, we decided this Bud was for us.

The business writer Paul Brent has tagged the year 1980 and the introduction of Budweiser to Canada as the beginning of the modern beer era in this country. Whatever Canadians said about the inherent worth of American beer, Budweiser was an instant hit, exceeding Labatt's expectations. By autumn of that year it had grabbed more than five percent of the Canadian market.

The very next year, Carling O'Keefe rolled out its own American brand, Miller High Life. Carling O'Keefe had never developed one or two powerhouse national brands the way Labatt and Molson had back in the 1950s, preferring instead to sell a relatively larger number of beers—O'Keefe, Carling, Dow, and Brading. With Miller, the company gained something similar to their rivals' national brands for the first time. Molson brought up the rear, making a deal with Coors to brew the famed "Colorado Kool-Aid" in Canada. The first batches of Canadian-brewed Coors appeared on shelves in Alberta and British Columbia on November 1, 1985, not even a month after the deal between the two companies had been announced.

All three of these American brands, brewed under licence agreements where the Canadian brewer split the profits with the American originator, were successful. It didn't hurt any of these beers that, long before they ever landed on Canadian shelves, most people here had at least heard of them. Canadian fans who followed sports on American television (and that was most of them) had been saturated for decades with ads for American brands. But that our belief in our own superiority vis-à-vis the United States (a central pillar of the English-Canadian identity) was so easily overcome in this one all-important area remains staggering.

Carling O'Keefe's Miller High Life may have been the second American beer launched in Canada, but it could claim its own distinction. Unlike Labatt, which had sold Budweiser in the standard brown Canadian stubby, Carling O'Keefe's Miller came in a clear glass, long-necked bottle, just like the American original. The stubby's days were suddenly numbered. By 1986, it would be gone as anything other than an occasional novelty nostalgia item.

So good it's made Canada
famous for beer
throughout the world

Now enjoyed in over 60 countries.

LEFT: *Black Label was drunk worldwide, but Carling O'Keefe had no real pan-Canadian brand.*

BELOW: *Combining two popular brands was a common marketing ploy.*

LEFT: *In 1973, Labatt's launched Cool Spring, Canada's first light beer.*

RIGHT: *Carling O'Keefe's Miller boasted American flavour, bottles, and good times.*

For the big Canadian brewers, the introduction of American beers kicked off two decades that can only be called the golden age of the gimmick. Back in the late 1970s, it seemed revolutionary when the breweries introduced light (or rather, "lite") versions of all their popular beers. Now change was constant. Labatt soon brought out the twist-top, which its competitors first dismissed and then quickly copied. The breweries also began to introduce an array of unusual products, including "dry" beers. Originally developed by the Japanese, dry beers were more thoroughly fermented than other brews, giving them a higher alcohol content, about 5.5 percent. The extra fermentation also meant that these dry beers had much less residual sweetness than other brews—critics described them as almost tasteless. Molson rolled out its first in 1989; Labatt followed fast. The next new product was draft beer in bottles. Labatt got off the mark first this time, when they brought out Genuine Draft in 1992. Molson quickly followed, bringing out Miller Genuine Draft (one of the American beers that had likely inspired Labatt) under licence, and going after Labatt through the courts.

No sooner had beer drinkers absorbed dry beers and draft beer in bottles, than they were confronted by "ice" beers. Now, there was a good deal

La bar shark.

The ingenious Dry campaign rattled off a series of "la" phrases, including "La batt."

BELOW: *Ice beers featured edgy black-and-silver graphics.*

of argument over what exactly constituted an ice beer, but essentially brewers make it by lowering the temperature of finished beer so that it begins to freeze, at which point the ice crystals are filtered out. Because water freezes at a warmer temperature than alcohol, this leaves behind a beer with a higher alcohol content—Molson's Black Ice is 6.1 percent, for example. (Rural tipplers lacking access to a still had long used the same technique to turn cider into the more powerful applejack.) Cold-filtering beer has another effect. With chilling, the protein in beer begins to coagulate into particles, to which tannins and hops then attach. The coagulated particles—and most of the beer's harsher flavours—are then filtered out of the final product.

You could pretty well sum up all these beers as high concept, low flavour. After the release of each new beer, an advertising campaign inevitably followed. Hoping to get a jump on the competition, each brewer tried to grab at least five percent of the market, and then repeated the process the next year. In the end, it

Labatt ICE BEER 5.6% alc./vol.

123

seemed as if the brewers were just playing mix-and-match with the concepts: maybe there wasn't a Genuine Dry, but how about Dry Ice?

SO MANY OF these gimmicks seemed silly at the time, but they were a sign of something troubling.

Put baldly, the big brewers were running out of beer drinkers. After decades of galloping postwar growth, by the 1980s the beer market was going as flat as a bottle of Export left out on the patio overnight. The bulge of baby boomers was working its way into adulthood. They were followed by, well, almost no one—it was the time of the baby bust. Brewers couldn't count on new customers just showing up. If they wanted to grow, they were going to have to steal market share.

Beer companies had introduced new brands in the past, of course. And not just the national brands of the 1950s. Carling O'Keefe had tried Charrington Toby in the 1960s, and then Heidelberg and Carlsberg in the 1970s. Labatt had gone with an attempt at what you might call a world beer in the late 1960s (Skol, which was brewed by a variety of brewers in different countries). These and others were successful to varying degrees. But historically beers were given a

Beer companies also experimented with new formats, such as aluminum cans.

The pint bottle was another short-lived attempt to grab consumer attention.

much longer time to make a mark—Blue took the better part of a decade to become number one. Flogging beer became a desperate and dizzying battle of all against all.

First to stumble was Carling O'Keefe. It was dogged by declining share, from 40 percent of the Canadian market in 1964 to 29 percent in 1983—and that was a good year, the one when they brought out Miller. Rothmans sold the lagging company to the Australian brewer Elders IXL in 1987. Carling lost the rights to brew Carlsberg, one of its few successful brands, when Elders IXL took them over. Unwilling to expend the money needed to turn it around, the Australian brewer promptly unloaded Carling O'Keefe by selling it to Molson. E.P. Taylor's monumental achievement became little more than a memory as brands like Red Cap were shut down, while others were assigned to a living death of unadvertised oblivion or turned into discount brands.

Taking over Carling O'Keefe gave Molson 53 percent of the market, but in the zero-growth, see-saw market of the 1990s, that edge was relatively short-lived. By 1992, after the introduction of their Genuine Draft, Labatt's share of the market had jumped by almost 2 percent, and Molson edged down to 50.3 percent. The Canadian beer market was coming to resemble the Western Front in 1917: two powerful enemies, each unable to defeat the other, but obliged to expend incredible resources just to remain deadlocked.

Regulatory changes were coming, too. Some were welcome—by the early 1990s, the old provincial trade barriers were coming down, which meant the companies no longer needed to have a brewery in every province in which

ABOVE: *Formosa Spring introduced draft beer in bottles—the holy grail of beer— in 1973.*

LEFT: *Labatt introduced theirs in 1992.*

When I think of Canada,
I think of

beautiful places

beautiful people

and the best beer I ever tasted. Labatt's.

"Welcome to the USA, Labatt's."

© Labatt Importers, Inc., Amherst, N.Y., 1978

Searching for growth in the late 1970s, Labatt looked to the United States.

they did business. They started rationalizing, shutting down plants, especially in the West, that operated at far below capacity. More ominously, the United States–Canada free trade pact became law in 1989, though the beer industry received a five-year exemption. As if it were a taste of things to come, that summer saw Ontario liquor stores flooded with cheap canned beer from the United States. Fights over access to each other's markets dragged on for a few years, but both sides finally opened up, and the Americans had free access to Canada (including Ontario's Brewers Retail stores) by 1993. To end-run the Americans, both big Canadian brewers introduced their own discount brands. Labatt created Wildcat, and Molson used the name of their now absorbed rival, Carling. Creating their own discount brands made sense, but it would have unpleasant side effects for them in the long run.

Labatt's solution to a flat market was to look outside Canada. In 1987, it had bought an American brewery, Pennsylvania's Latrobe Brewing Company. Latrobe made the legendary Rolling Rock, which had a strong supporting role in Michael Cimino's film *The Deer Hunter* as the only beer that Robert De Niro and his friends ever drank. Unfortunately, Labatt's agreement with Budweiser prohibited them from selling the cult beer in Canada.

Labatt looked farther afield. It launched Labatt Lager in the United Kingdom, through a deal with a brewer there, and then bought two Italian breweries, Birra Moretti and Prinz Brau, in 1990. Alas, Labatt's other ambitions for expansion outside North America were not so successful: Guinness outbid them to buy Spain's Cruz del Campo, and the price tag for Australia's Bond Brewing—upwards of $1.8 billion—was just too high.

Labatt looked south next, to Mexico, buying into the Mexican brewer FEMSA Cerveza SA, maker of such notable brands as Tecate, Dos Equis, and Sol. The company paid $720 million, which gave them 22 percent of the Mexican beer maker. They planned ultimately to expand their stake to 30 percent. Mexico boasted three times the population of Canada but only two brewers. Best of all, Mexicans were young: half the population was under the age of nineteen, with their best beer-drinking years ahead of them. It was the baby boom all over again.

Then everything went pear-shaped. In December 1994, the peso collapsed, and Mexico entered a full-on economic crisis. Labatt had to write off hundreds of millions of dollars in the value of its investment in FEMSA. In the late 1980s, the Canadian conglomerate Brascan had bought a large stake in Labatt, and encouraged its expansion. Unfortunately for Labatt, Brascan dumped its share in 1993. The new shareholders, already wary of the company's performance, now became downright alarmed. Labatt was suddenly a takeover target, and wound up in the embrace of the Belgian brewer Interbrew in 1995.

Molson's management tried a different approach. To keep the company growing in the face of a flat beer market they would diversify. This they proceeded to do—with chaotic results. Their then president, Marshall A. "Mickey" Cohen, concluded that an excellent candidate for growth was a small cleaning chemical company that Molson had bought in the late seventies named Diversey. Cohen merged Diversey with a large American chemical company named DuBois, but Diversey took Molson to the cleaners, bleeding their bottom line for three years before being dumped in 1995. An attempt to create a Canadian equivalent of Home Depot out of its Beaver lumber stores was equally short-lived.

The company's success in the complex American market was mixed at best.

THE *Moosehead* STORY

FACED WITH growing competition from the big three and hamstrung by regulations that made expansion in Canada almost impossible, New Brunswick's Moosehead chose another way to survive—by looking south.

Until the early 1970s, Atlantic Canada had stayed largely outside the grip of the big three. Newfoundland had lost its independent breweries in the early 1960s, but elsewhere the region was still dominated by local firms, Oland's in Halifax and Moosehead in Saint John. The firms were run by separate (and largely estranged) branches of the Oland family.

Fearing what seemed inevitable, the Halifax Olands sold out to Labatt in 1971.

Facing a flat local market and deep-pocketed competitors, Moosehead might have met a similar fate. But as Harvey Sawler explains in *Last Canadian Beer,* his book on Moosehead, an opportunity found the firm. Paul Lohmeyer, chair of the American beer distributor All Brand Importers, was a man always looking for new products to introduce into the United States. Canadian beer enjoyed a high reputation with Americans, and he was eager to get his hands on a new brew from north of the border.

Derek Oland, son of then chairman P.W. Oland, was enthusiastic about Lohmeyer's pitch to sell their beer in the United States, but his father and the rest of the firm's management was not. It took Paul Lohmeyer and Derek Oland three years to convince Moosehead's skeptics that this was the way to go.

Initially, management at Moosehead thought that their Alpine brand would logically be the first beer to sell in the United States. Lohmeyer, however, had other

ideas. He knew that what would sell in the United States was the idea of Canada, a land of lakes and pine forests—ideas nicely encapsulated in a beer called Moosehead. They would emphasize this. To that end, even Moosehead's label was redesigned, to make it look somehow more authentically "Canadian."

Lohmeyer and the Olands also agreed to position Moosehead as a premium import, more like Heineken than Red Cap, Golden, or the other Canadian beers that had been sold in the United States before.

All Brand Importers released Moosehead in the United States in 1978. Although they couldn't afford much major advertising, All Brand built the beer's profile through store displays, advertisements in trade publications, and exposure in bars.

Thanks to the quality of the beer and the smarts of its American distributor, Moosehead was a success, especially among the preppies of the Northeast. At its peak Moosehead sold six million cases in a single year.

Moosehead's sales in the United States are down from those levels today, but the company's successful launch there had important repercussions. The brand's success south of the border got it better known in the rest of Canada—even before it could be bought in most provinces other than New Brunswick. When provincial barriers came down in 1992, Moosehead was ready to expand. From a beleaguered regional company, Moosehead was transformed into a national player in Canada. By the end of the first decade of the twenty-first century, Moosehead would be the fourth-largest brewer in Canada, and the largest one in the country not in foreign hands.

FACING PAGE AND ABOVE: *Moosehead's look was a big hit with Americans.*

BELOW: *Derek Oland (right) with his son Andrew, Moosehead's current president.*

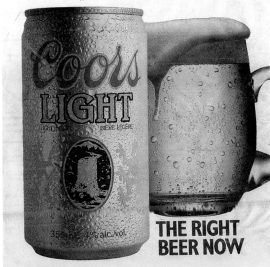

The Silver Bullet™

Now's the time to catch the bright, refreshing taste of Coors Light—Canada's most popular light beer.

Coors LIGHT

THE RIGHT BEER NOW

Sigh. By the early twenty-first century, a light American beer was our number two brand.

Molson didn't fare much better when it concentrated on its core business. In 1993, the company announced that it had sold a 20 percent share in Molson to Miller Brewing in the United States. They hoped this would give Molson's products better access to American markets. It did for a time at least, but it also succeeded in riling Coors, which felt that the deal with Miller violated the agreement it had with Molson to brew beers in Canada. An arbitration panel ruled that Molson had done Coors wrong, and ordered the Montreal brewer to pay $100 million in damages and $15 million in costs. Frantic to keep a bestseller, Molson paid Miller $201 million to back out of its deal in December 1997. Molson negotiated a new deal with Coors, which now held 50.1 percent of a new joint venture called Coors Canada.

You have to wonder about Canadian beer companies. The minute they have trouble keeping their sales up, they seek out a tempestuous Latin partner. Labatt had FEMSA; now, Molson decided on Brazil. Late in 2000, they purchased the Bavaria beer brand, a popular Brazilian lager; in March 2001, they announced that they had bought the country's second-largest brewer, Cervejarias Kaiser. Together these two companies gave them 18 percent of the Brazilian market. But Brazilians didn't display the loyalty of Molson's North American customers; when the brewer raised prices, their Brazilian drinkers quickly shifted to other brands. A different culture, an unstable currency, fickle customers, and cutthroat competition all hurt Molson. By 2004, their Brazilian market share had fallen to 10 percent. In 2006, they unloaded 58 percent of their holdings in Cervejarias Kaiser.

As the 1990s gave way to the twenty-first century, both Labatt and Molson found themselves in the same tough spot. As Canada's two remaining big breweries, they were still rich, but they had lost the high ground. Increasingly, their bestselling beers weren't ones they had created or brewed under licence, but those they distributed for their foreign owners or partners: Stella Artois and Beck in the case of Labatt, Heineken and Corona for Molson. These new imports did well and made them money—but nothing like what they once coined off their traditional powerhouse brands, whose market these upstarts were stealing.

At the opposite end of the spectrum, Molson and Labatt had pioneered discount brands in the 1990s, but they soon saw themselves usurped by the likes of Ontario's Lakeport Brewing, the famed buck-a-beer folks. Says Bob Scott, who runs the Toronto-based brewery consulting firm Ascot Marketing, "Beer drinkers have been trained to look for the best deal. Price is king now." From 1996 on, after successively jacking prices throughout the nineties to boost revenue, the big breweries began putting their flagship brands on sale to win market share. Labatt's parent company bought out Lakeport in 2006, but the damage had been done. Canadian beer companies found themselves in a position analogous to that of the old department stores. While the high and low ends survived, the middle was being squeezed out.

Gimmicks didn't save Carling O'Keefe and they weren't enough for Labatt and Molson either.

WHEN THE END finally came, few of us really noticed.

Throughout the summer of 2004, the business sections were filled with reports of the impending on-again, off-again merger of the American brewing giant Coors and the sole surviving big Canadian-owned brewery, Molson. Molson executives were quick to point out that what they planned was not a sale; it was, rather, a marriage of equals, which would create synergies that would help this new North American behemoth compete in a nasty global marketplace. The family squabbled but in the end, in February 2005, the company's shareholders went for the deal. It felt almost anticlimactic. The

Molson chairman Eric Molson (left) and Coors head Leo Kiely announce the merger, July 22, 2004.

new Molson Coors was the third-largest brewer in the United States and the fifth-largest in the world, with fifteen breweries and 14,800 employees in four countries. Not long after the merger, the new company abandoned Molson's long-running "I AM CANADIAN" advertising campaign, and the symbolism was not lost.

Anyone who had followed the story couldn't have helped feeling a sense of déjà vu a little over two years later. In the fall of 2007, the American business pages were full of news about a planned marriage of equals between Coors and Miller. Left unmentioned in all these stories was Coors's earlier "equal partner." Now it seemed that wherever the American firm went, Molson went, too.

It was the end of an era. Not just the modern era of Canadian brewing that began with Budweiser, but something bigger, something stretching right back to the late eighteenth century. And as if to rub it in, the final merger between the two American big guys went through on June 30, 2008—the day before Canada Day. The date was ironic, perhaps, but it would not stand out in Canadian beer-drinking history. We already had enough of these sad milestones, and New Brunswick's plucky upstart Moosehead was left as the largest Canadian-owned brewery.

Other less grandiose, but no less disturbing, changes were afoot. Molson and Labatt's key brands, the beers that almost defined the Canadian beer drinking experience, had been toppled from their positions of dominance. For example, in February 2008, the *Globe and Mail* reported that Budweiser was now Labatt's number one seller, accounting for 12 percent of the Canadian beer market, while Blue, formerly the company's top performer, held onto a much smaller 5 percent.

The takeover of Labatt by Interbrew had been a generally positive affair. But in 2004, when Interbrew amalgamated with the Brazilian AmBev to create InBev (now Anheuser-Busch InBev), the world's largest brewer, things changed. Owing to its location in the New World, Labatt fell under the control of the Brazilians, a notoriously unsentimental crew.

David Kincaid, a former VP at Labatt during the 1990s beer wars and later an executive at Interbrew who now runs his own brand consulting business in Toronto, thinks this may seal Labatt's fate. "If I had to look out over the next five or ten years, Labatt will not exist," he said to me in an interview. There will be sales offices, Kincaid thinks, but no breweries. Things look grim for his former competitor, too. In 2008, Kincaid said, "I don't see the Molson name disappearing [as long as Molson is still CEO]. But the role of the brands within their portfolio—Canadian has been protected as its own little thing within Molson Coors—I don't see that lasting." What effect Eric Molson's retirement in May 2009 will have on the company remains to be seen. And we haven't seen the end of the amalgamations in the brewing world internationally, either, Kincaid says.

Sad, sure, but remember: life on Earth didn't end when the dinosaurs died out. Even before they roared their last, newer, more nimble creatures were taking their place—warm-blooded mammals, our ancestors. Even as the beer titans faded, exciting new life forms were arising.

Steelback was businessman Frank Angelo's failed bid to create a major new brewery.

8

THE NEW GUYS

*Like tasteless white bread and the universal cardboard
hamburger, the new beer is produced for the tasteless common
denominator. It must not offend anyone anywhere.
Corporate beer is not too heavy, not too bitter, not too alcoholic,
not too malty. In other words, corporate beer reduces
every characteristic that makes beer beer.*

THESE WORDS belong to Frank Appleton, a former quality control super-
visor for O'Keefe who had turned to freelance writing. They were published in the May/June 1978 issue of *Harrowsmith* magazine. Canadians have
never much gone in for brash political declarations or manifestos, but you could
call Appleton's piece the Canadian beer drinkers' declaration of independence.

They needed it. Of Mr. and Ms. Canadian beer drinker of the 1970s,
you could say that their taste buds may have been born free, but they
were everywhere in chains. The old breweries and varieties—the ones,

< *Fritz Maytag surrounded by his crew at Anchor Brewing, 1978.*

Appleton said, "that once gave this country an international reputation"—were gone, swallowed by the big three (ultimately the big two). "Fervoured TV commercials to the contrary," Appleton lamented that now,

> the stage has been reached where all the big breweries are making virtually the same product, with different names and labels.

Frank Appleton hadn't set out to write a manifesto, at least not entirely. His ostensible purpose was to explain to people who were as fed up with corporate beer as he was how to make their own. That was something he knew well as a trained brewer. Not many people brewed at home in the 1970s, and it wasn't always easy to learn how or to find the right ingredients.

But *Harrowsmith* had reach. By the late 1970s, when Appleton's piece appeared, the magazine had a Canadian circulation of more than 100,000 copies an issue, making it the eighth-largest magazine in Canada. Very few of its readers were actual back-to-the-landers; most were affluent young urbanites who had been touched by sixties sensibilities. A piece championing the merits of traditional beer using old-fashioned ingredients found a ready audience among them.

Appleton's tirade against corporate brewers echoed events occurring elsewhere in the English-speaking world. Just a few years earlier, four young Englishmen—Graham Lees, Bill Mellor, Michael Hardman, and Jim Makin—had gone on a holiday in the west of Ireland. They soon discovered, says Hardman, "that there wasn't much to drink there. No ale." One day the conversation turned to the general decline of beer in Britain. Like Canada's, British brewing had undergone rounds of consolidation, amalgamations, and closings over the previous decades, many of them due to none other than E.P. Taylor who, having built

Frank Appleton (centre) is the father of Canadian microbrewing.

Canadian Breweries, had jumped the Atlantic in search of new worlds to conquer. By the mid-1960s, six big brewers held more than 90 percent of the U.K. market—including ownership of hundreds of pubs that pushed bland, homogeneous beer on their customers. These modern, pasteurized, and artificially carbonated beers, called keg ales, were rapidly supplanting the old real ales, the unpasteurized, unfiltered beers that fermented in the barrel. Then and there, the four young Englishmen hit upon the idea of a "Campaign for the Revitalisation of Ale," which quite nicely abbreviated to CAMRA. A year later, the four of them got together with some other friends in a pub in the north of England and held their first meeting. (Not too long after this, CAMRA took on the name that it bears today, the Campaign for Real Ale.)

CAMRA had been a movement literally waiting to happen. Soon, knowledgeable amateurs and other beer fanatics were flocking to join. Says Hardman, "We grew from 1,000 members after two years to 25,000 members after three." CAMRA held beer festivals, and put out a pub guide, which

The CAMRA men: Jim Makin, Bill Mellor, Michael Hardman, and Graham Lees.

TOP: *Fritz Maytag at work.*

ABOVE: *John Mitchell, left, and Frank Appleton.*

they still publish. It's no exaggeration to say that CAMRA revitalized British beer. In 1971, says Hardman, Britain had around 150 breweries—there are about 500 today.

There were other interesting developments closer to Canada. In 1965, Fritz Maytag (scion of the washing machine dynasty) had taken over a failing company in San Francisco named Anchor Brewing. Anchor was small—it produced about six hundred barrels a year—and it had a deservedly terrible reputation for bad beer. But Maytag started learning everything he could about the business of brewing. After buying out his business partner in 1969, Maytag came up with a revolutionary idea—he would brew traditional beer, using malt made from two-row barley, with no adjuncts, and real hops, not extract. As Maureen Ogle put it in her history of American brewing, *Ambitious Brew*, Maytag had realized something: "Out there was an audience eager for authenticity." Small-scale brewers would soon be springing up all over the United States.

What happened in Canada was a series of random events and coincidences that would seem far-fetched if you saw them in a movie.

Forward to 1981 and a bar named the Troller Pub in Horseshoe Bay in West Vancouver. John Mitchell, the pub's proprietor, had been impressed on a recent trip to England by a visit to the country's surviving pub-breweries. Mitchell wanted to start one in Canada, but didn't know where to begin. He was lamenting this fact to a customer one day—who just happened to remember reading the piece in *Harrowsmith*. Mitchell tracked down Appleton and told his fellow English expatriate what he wanted. Appleton told him that he could certainly design the equipment, have it built, and teach Mitchell and his staff how to use it, but selling their beer would be another thing altogether. They would need a brewing licence from the province's Liquor Control and Licensing Branch. Appleton knew from dealing with them when he worked for O'Keefe that their favourite word was "no." He, Appleton, would help Mitchell to write an application, but cautioned him that it might take years for it to grind through the bureaucracy.

That same year, Premier Bill Bennett appointed Peter Hyndman as the province's minister of consumer and corporate affairs. One of Hyndman's first actions as minister was to deregulate the price of beer, which had historically been set by the Liquor Control and Licensing Branch. In theory deregulation would benefit the customer, by freeing the brewers to compete with one another on price. Instead, the big three all took advantage of the opportunity to raise their prices. And, by an astounding coincidence, all three boosted them by exactly the same amount.

Hyndman was furious but hamstrung. Deregulation meant he couldn't force them to lower their prices. Pressured by a journalist as to what exactly he could do to benefit consumers, Hyndman mentioned

John Mitchell and his son Edward hold their first pints from the Horseshoe Bay Brewery.

a recent application the board had received for a new idea—what was referred to then as a "cottage brewery." As Appleton tells the story now, on their next visit to the Vancouver offices of the Liquor Control and Licensing Branch, the province's bureaucrats couldn't have been friendlier or more eager to help. In June 1982, just six months after applying, the Horseshoe Bay Brewery had its brewing licence and had set up for business next door to the Troller Pub. Appleton would go on to design and install many other cottage breweries and what would soon be known as microbreweries over the next twenty years.

IT WAS AS if a door had been pushed open.

Leading the way, British Columbia saw a number of other cottage breweries open in 1983, and that same year work started in Vancouver on what would be the first truly Canadian microbrewery. The Granville Island Brewing Company constructed a five-thousand-barrel-capacity plant in the trendy Vancouver locale from which it took its name, at a cost of about $1.5 million,

and in the spring of 1984, started selling an unpasteurized, natural-ingredient lager in bottles and on draft.

December 1984 saw the opening of Canada's second microbrewery, the Brick Brewing Company, located in Waterloo, Ontario. In early 1985, Alberta gained its first micro, Big Rock Brewing. Both are still going today. After that there seemed to be a new brewery launching somewhere in the country about as fast as you could open a new beer: Hanshaus Brewery in New Brunswick, Golden Lion in Quebec, Conners in Ontario, and Strath-cona and Drummond in Alberta, all in 1986; B.C.'s Shaftebury and Ontario's Creemore Springs in 1987; future national powerhouse Slee-man Brewing & Malting in 1988. All in, forty-four new breweries opened between 1984 and 1989.

What these micros brewed—and brew—varied widely. Situated in the most "lager-positive" province of Canada, Alberta's Big Rock took a

LEFT: *Big Rock brewed ales and porters to win market in lager-crazy Alberta.*

FACING PAGE, TOP: *Granville Island's smart Vancouver brewery/pub.*

FACING PAGE, BOTTOM: *Granville draft tower.*

contrarian tack, initially brewing traditional ale, stout, and porter. Toronto's Conners and Guelph's Wellington (founded in 1987) created true British-style, cask-conditioned ales, unpasteurized and unfiltered. Toronto's Upper Canada made much of its adherence to the famed Bavarian "purity" laws, or *Reinheitsgebot,* that stated that beer could contain only malted barley (and later, malted wheat), hops, and water (and of course yeast, had those long-ago Bavarians but known of its importance). Vancouver's Granville Island made similar claims.

These new brewers brought back beers that had vanished from the Canadian scene long ago. When Upper Canada started making a wheat beer in the early 1990s, for example, it was the first time in a century this beer had been brewed in Ontario. The microbrewers introduced new beers, too, ones that were previously unknown here. Beers made with raspberries or even pumpkin.

In Quebec, Unibroue can take credit for creating a distinctive brewing tradition suitable for that province's distinct society. In 1991, Quebec businessman André Dion took over a failing microbrewery in Lennoxville in the Eastern Townships, renamed it Unibroue, and shifted it to Chambly, Quebec, about twenty kilometres south of Montreal. He took his new brewery in

WHEAT Beer

ALTHOUGH BEERS made with wheat have occasionally been brewed in Canada since the late eighteenth century (when he couldn't get barley to malt in his first brewing season, John Molson made use of it), the widespread acceptance of Belgian-style wheat (or white or wit beers, they are all the same thing) has really been a side effect of the explosion in craft brewing in Canada in the past twenty-five years.

Wheat beers are in some ways paradoxical brews. For one thing, they are not exclusively made of wheat. Instead, unmalted wheat is usually combined with malted barley. Making beer with nothing but wheat as the source of the sugars for the yeast would actually be quite messy. Not having much of a husk, wheat tends to leave behind a sloppy mush in the mash tun after it has been boiled to make wort.

Other details contribute to wheat beer's unique thirst-quenching taste. The Belgians typically flavour their wheat beers with Curaçao, orange peel, coriander, and other spices, which give them a sweeter fruity taste to go with their slightly lower alcohol content. People sometimes complement these flavours by drinking wheat beer with an orange slice. Visually speaking, one of the most distinctive elements of wheat beers is their cloudy appearance. Although they are made, like lagers, with a top-brewing yeast, historically they were not stored in cool caverns until they had fermented and the particles in the beer had settled. Instead, they were bottled relatively quickly and yeast was added to the bottles, to kick off a secondary fermentation. The result of this added yeast was a cloudy beer, much murkier than what we have seen in recent years.

Wheat beers represent a very different tradition in brewing than we are used to in Canada. Quebec's Unibroue was the first to brew them here, and it became almost *de rigueur* for every Quebec microbrewery (at least those run by French

speakers) to produce their own version. The style spread outside Quebec: Toronto's Mill Street Brewery and Garrison in Nova Scotia are just two microbreweries outside the province that now produce them. Thanks to their Belgian connection, Labatt has been selling Hoegaarden, arguably the most popular wheat beer in the world, in Canada for several years. In 2009, you might say that wheat beer "crossed over" or went mainstream when Alexander Keith rolled out its version, called Keith's Premium White, backed by a serious advertising campaign.

a completely different direction, contacting a Belgian brewer of live yeast beers and setting up a deal to use their recipes in Quebec. These almost fruity beers are made with wheat and then given a secondary fermentation after bottling, which gives them their distinctively cloudy appearance. They caught on quickly, permanently influencing the Quebec microbrews that followed. One notable fan of Unibroue's beers was the great Quebec rock star of the 1960s, Robert Charlebois. He became an investor in and vice-president of the company in 1993.

Having a rock star as vice-president might seem improbable, but Charlebois was not all that unlikely. There was no real career path for microbrewers, at least in the early stages. Calgary's Ed McNally, founder of Big Rock, was a lawyer turned barley farmer turned microbrewer. Jim Brickman of the Brick Brewing Company had a background in marketing. Peter McAuslan, founder of McAuslan in Montreal, had been a senior administrator at Dawson College, a Montreal-area CEGEP. McAuslan was also an enthusiastic amateur brewer, as was Bruce Cornish, one of the founders of Ontario's Great Lakes Brewing Company. John Sleeman and his wife had run an English-style pub before joining forces with his father-in-law to create a company to import beer. Sleeman, however, was unaware of his family's brewing history until in 1984 his aunt gave him a bottle from the old brewery—and his grandfather's recipe book. What united these people and drew them into brewing was a mixture of passion and faith.

This emotional commitment often wasn't always enough. Overly optimistic projections could backfire. Conners Brewing, for example, assumed initial sales in their first year of 450,000 litres, all without the benefit of advertising. Their actual sales for that first year were two-thirds that, putting them $500,000 in debt on revenues of under $1 million. The company never really recovered and was ultimately purchased by Brick.

Balancing the need for money against the need for control could also be a problem for these upstarts. When it was founded in 1985, Toronto's Upper Canada Brewing was well capitalized, but by 1991, when it needed more money to grow, founder Frank Heaps didn't feel he could call on his initial investors again. Banks were nervous, however, obliging Heaps to look elsewhere. What followed was a chain of events that led to the firm's slipping from his control into the hands of Hurlow Partners and the Ontario Teachers' Pension Plan. Heaps, who had resigned as president but stayed on the company's board, railed against the direction that the majority shareholders were taking the company in, but to no avail. After several years of losses, Upper Canada was sold to Sleeman in February 1998. Their plant was closed, and production moved to the Sleeman's brewery near Guelph.

Often, too, the little breweries were victims of circumstances beyond their control. When Ontario's Brewers Retail stores started selling imported beer in 1994 (previously you'd had to go to a liquor store to get it), that hurt that province's micros. And a lot of micros nationwide were hurt by the decision of the Brewers Assocation of Canada in 1994 to bring in a new standard bottle, a long-necked, brown glass affair designed to take twist-off caps and be reusable, just like the old stubby. Many microbrewers had their own custom bottles, which were often one of the few forms of advertising they could afford; others didn't use glass at all, favouring plastic one-litre bottles. Now they would either have to switch to the

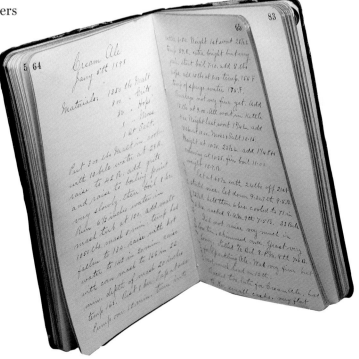

FACING PAGE, TOP: *John Sleeman raises a glass.*

FACING PAGE, BOTTOM: *Big Rock's Ed McNally.*

BELOW: *Getting his grandfather's recipe book inspired Sleeman's brewing career.*

Lord of the rings.

The new look of John Labatt Classic.
Brewed to be the best of the best.

Launched in 1983, Labatt Classic was about as good as it gets from the big breweries.

new standard bottles or pay a sorting fee. Sleeman's, which had adopted a clear glass bottle for all its products, based on the historic bottle that John Sleeman had been given by his aunt, opted to pay the fee. Upper Canada did likewise, until being tagged with a million-dollar bill by Brewers Retail. They then switched to the new Industry Standard Bottle, at a cost of $2 million. For many small breweries, there was no good choice. Ontario's Algonquin Brewery, for example, squeezed by foreign beers on the one side and the new bottle on the other, was forced out of business.

A CYNICAL BEER drinker might conclude that the new standard bottle was the crafty means the mainstream or "macro" brewers had chosen to hobble their upstart competitors. This would be unfair. The big two didn't think badly of the microbreweries.

They didn't think of them at all.

Was it arrogance? Not really. Read early articles or interviews with the first microbrewers and you'll come across a joke that came up time and again: "Molson spills more than we make." There was an element of truth to it, too. In the eighties or early nineties, when the first micros were opening up, their production and their possible share of the market hardly seemed worth worrying about. The definition of a microbrewery in those days was one that brewed less than 20,000 hectolitres a year (a hectolitre equals about 12.2 cases of twenty-four). Any of the big three's breweries could turn that out in a month. In a feature on CBC's *The Journal* on September 26, 1986, on what was then the very new phenomenon of the microbrewery, Molson's Barry Joslin put forth what might be called the corporate line:

Most of the consumption patterns indicate that the market is moving towards a product that is lighter, [and] somewhat sweeter. This is happening not just in Canada but in other countries as well. And I guess like in any consumer product industry there's always going to be a group of people that wants to retain the original qualities of the product... And I think the micros in many respects meet that need. It's not reflective of a general trend. In some ways it's a reaction to a general trend.

To some extent of course the big brewers were driving this trend, but their own experiences suggested that they were right. Well into the 1970s, the then big three pumped out stouts and porters, even though the total audience for these beers had declined to around one percent of the market by the mid-1960s (admittedly the companies did virtually nothing to market them). Later attempts at introducing beers that deviated from mainstream taste were not successful. In 1977, Labatt, always the more daring of the big brewers, tried to bring out a new dark beer called Grand Prix Ale. Bill White, a former brewmaster with the company, says it was a "heavy malt ale" that was "about the shortest-lived beer of all time. It was brought out that summer and fall and then discontinued. People just weren't buying the dark beers." The company's new higher-end premium beer, John Labatt Classic, introduced in 1983, did do better.

Labatt also made a stab at repositioning IPA, including fitting it out with a snazzy embossed bottle. It was, says White, "all malt, great hops, fully flavoured." But it didn't find a new audience and in 1993, after 125 years of production, Labatt pulled the plug on it.

Instead, the big brewers focused on what they knew: the advertising-driven national brands, and a range of what might be called "novelty" beers—the drys, the ices, and so forth. Dan O'Neill, Molson's president in the 1990s,

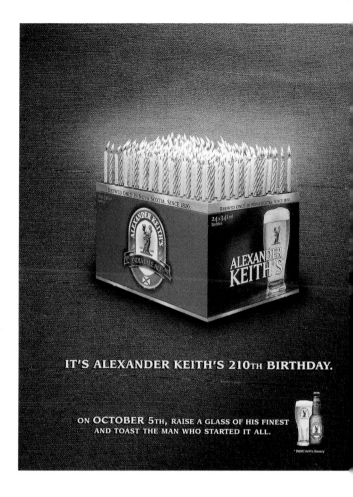

IT'S ALEXANDER KEITH'S 210TH BIRTHDAY.

ON OCTOBER 5TH, RAISE A GLASS OF HIS FINEST AND TOAST THE MAN WHO STARTED IT ALL.

Labatt positioned Alexander Keith's carefully, giving it some of a micro's feel.

147

Labatt's Duffy's was another attempt to tap into the micro market.

once dismissed the micros as "mosquitoes or blackflies buzzing around your head."

The micros might not have had much of the market, probably not even five percent in the 1990s (even including the so-called regional brewers like Moosehead and Sleeman). But in a market that was generally flat, this was the only segment that was growing. What those so-called blackflies and mosquitoes had *did* look awfully tantalizing. The big brewers started trying to poach it.

With indifferent results. In late fall 1993, Molson announced its new Signature Series, which featured two beers touted as preservative-free and brewed from recipes more than two hundred years old. "Dare to be great" was the tagline used in the ads for Molson Amber Lager and Molson Cream Ale. There was nothing wrong with these beers; but as Allen Sneath puts it in *Brewed In Canada*, although they were "well received at a level that would be acceptable to any microbrewery, they did not deliver the market share Molson expects from its heavily advertised brands..." The company quickly dropped them. Molson's next attempt, in the spring of 1994, was Red Dog, which featured a label bearing a glowering cartoonish red bull dog—but no mention of a brewery. Red Dog was positioned as being somehow "edgy" and "alternative"; by the fall of 1994, it was more commonly referred to as "Dead Dog" and quickly interred. Labatt tried and failed with Duffy's Dark Lager, available only in draft, though the wheat beer it brought out in the nineties is still around. But after their early failures, both brewers finally managed to make some inroads. Molson brought out Rickard's Red, a beer purported to be brewed by something called the Capilano Brewing Company, which was in fact the original name for Molson's Vancouver plant, bought back in the 1950s. Labatt managed a similar sort of positioning with Alexander Keith's, which the company's clever marketing minds positioned as a scrappy little independent brewery down Halifax way. (Labatt had picked up the Alexander Keith brand when it purchased Oland in 1971. Oland had bought the venerable brewer back in 1927.) To grab more of the micro market, Molson bought a piece of Brick Brewing in 1997, and all of Ontario's Creemore Springs in April 2005, which it has so far left largely alone. (In the fall of 2009, Creemore/Molson bought Granville Island.) Sleeman, now so large as to be more properly termed a macro rather than a micro, kept its hand in the micro end by buying Unibroue in 2004. But so far none of this nibbling at the margins of microbrewing has discouraged truly independent small brewers.

THIRTY YEARS AFTER Appleton penned his screed, Canadian beer drinking has been utterly transformed. As of the middle part of the decade, the Canadian Association of Small Brewers, the micros' umbrella group, boasted ninety members, who together now account for five percent of the market. That seems small, especially compared with the big brewers, but in today's

BELOW LEFT:
A cork-top bottle from Unibroue, a popular Quebec firm.

BELOW RIGHT:
Les Brasseurs du Nord's Boréale line focused on ales, Quebec's traditional preference.

fractured marketplace, it is far from inconsequential. As many people (maybe more) now drink microbrewery beers as drink Blue, once the undisputed champion of Canadian corporate beer. Some venerable microbreweries have disappeared, and others have been bought. But new ones continue to spring up. Creating a new microbrewery is still not a terribly expensive or difficult endeavour. Rob Creighton, the brewmaster at Cambridge's Grand River Brewery, has helped over the years to set up a number of micro- (and not-so-micro-) breweries. He told me that to create one today would take about a million dollars –$500,000 for equipment, location, and raw materials, and another $500,000 to cover any unforeseen problems. Once annual production hits 1,300 hectolitres, says Creighton, the operation should be in the black.

The revolution in brewing has touched every part of Canada. You don't need to live in Toronto, Montreal, or Vancouver to benefit. New Brunswick's liquor board, for example, carries thirty-five separate craft beers, including pale ales, raspberry wheat beers, bitters, and London-style porters. No less than fifteen of those are produced by two micros located in New Brunswick: Pump House in Moncton and Picaroons in Fredericton.

Beau's bottle (below left) recalls the reusable "growlers" of the past (below right).

TRY A WELLY ON

WELLINGTON
BREWERY

India Pale Ale

Inspirée de la côte est, elle est parsemée d'amertume et d'arômes du houblon sur un fond de malt. Cette bière peut changer légèrement d'une cuvée à l'autre à mesure que nous explorons les diverses interprétations de ce style.

Return for refund where applicable. Consigné là où la loi le prescrit.
Northampton Brewing Co. Ltd Fredericton, New Brunswick

India Pale Ale

An East Coast-style India Pale Ale that weaves intense hop bitterness and aroma throughout a blanket of malt background. This beer may change slightly from batch to batch as we explore the various interpretations of the style.

PICAROONS

Bière   Ale

YIPPEE IPA

6.5% alc./vol. • 500 mL

ABOVE: *Ontario's Wellington has developed a range of Wellington-themed material.*

LEFT AND BELOW: *Picaroons whimsical labels put the mainstream brewers to shame.*

Stout traditionnelle

La stout classique irlandaise sert de fond à cet élixir aromatique noirâtre; or des variations sont possibles d'une cuvée à l'autre, le résultat savoureux de l'aventure improvisée.

Return for refund where applicable. Consigné là où la loi le prescrit.
Northampton Brewing Co. Ltd Fredericton, New Brunswick

Traditional Stout

The classic Irish-style dry stout is the basic background of this aromatic ebony elixir but deviations may occur from batch to batch as we improvisationally wander through variations on the theme.

PICAROONS

Bière   Ale

TIMBER HOG

5% alc./vol. • 500 mL

Microbreweries have succeeded by their attention to the particular. Those corporate beers that Appleton vilified were an attempt to purge beer of its specifics; craft beers brought them back. To turn Appleton's words on their head, a craft beer might offend someone—they could find it too heavy, or too bitter, or too alcoholic, or too malty. Or they might find it really interesting. Whatever the major breweries thought about long-term trends in brewing, the micros now play a greater role in setting them than the big two. In the spring of 2009, when Alexander Keith's brought out both a wheat beer and a dark ale, it was an obvious case of a big brewer playing catch-up on changing taste trends.

The microbreweries' particularity isn't limited to just their beer. It also comes through in funky bottles, beautiful labels, and fresh graphics. And even where the beer is brewed—old churches, railway roundhouses, and Victorian storefronts. Most of all it comes through in a local approach. Canadian

Toronto's Steam Whistle Brewery boasts a fleet of vintage delivery vehicles.

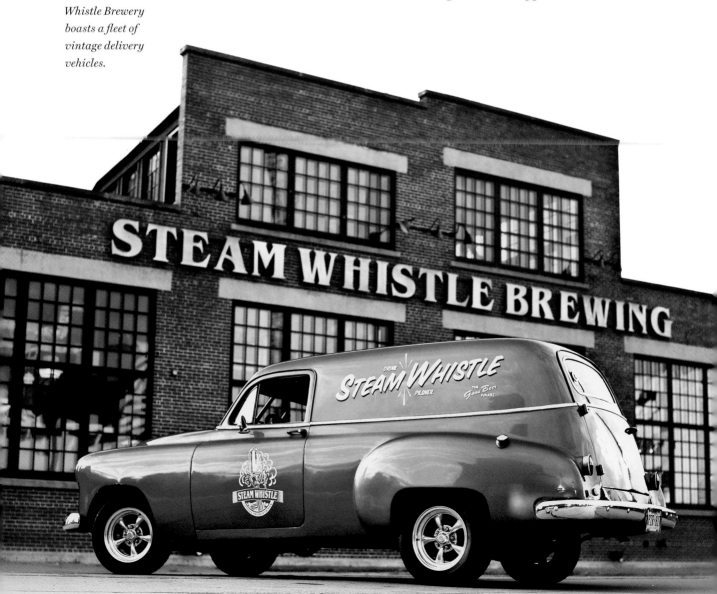

brewing was historically very regional; the micros brought it back to that. Alberta's Big Rock is a direct reference to a local landform, the famed 16,500-metric-ton Okotoks erratic, a boulder dropped off millennia ago by a retreating glacier; Unibroue's brands and labels have their roots in Quebec life and folklore; Quidi Vidi could come only from St. John's. This is the age of local food and the 100-Mile Diet; the microbreweries fit right into it. Prohibited by costs from pursuing more traditional advertising, the microbreweries forge tight relationships with their potential drinkers through sponsoring local events, often creating special event labels for their beers to publicize them. McAuslan does Montreal's Just for Laughs Festival, Steam Whistle backs indie music, and Granville Island does the Vancouver International Jazz Festival.

More micros may come into existence, or current ones may consolidate, but however the market shakes out, the demand for their product—for different and unusual beers, using good ingredients and made in relatively small batches—can only increase. Distinct beers are part of our way of life now. No one thinks it odd to go to a beer tasting or learn which ale goes best with which food. Out in Vancouver, where the trend began, Walter Cosman, the general manager of the Granville Island Brewery, says the micros' share of the Vancouver market in 2009 was up to 8 or 9 percent. (South of the border, says Cosman, micros do even better: "In Portland [the share] is well over 20 percent.")

What's next? If developments in the United Kingdom and the United States are anything to go by, it'll likely be growth in what could be termed "extreme" brewing. That could follow the sort of rule-breaking, no-holds-barred beer making pioneered by the Delaware-based Dogfish Head Craft Brewery's Sam Calagione, creator of such brews as 90 Minute IPA and Midas Touch. (The latter is a nine-percent-alcohol brew based on ingredients found

Today's micros are as proudly regional as the breweries of a century ago.

153

Women watch the bottling line at Creemore Springs' plant in Ontario.

in ancient drinking vessels taken from the tomb of King Midas.) Or brewers might take their lead from Scotland's BrewDog. Impressed by how much their customers knew about beer, starting in November 2008 BrewDog's twenty-something co-owners invited visitors to their website to help them create "a beer by the people for the people!" by voting on what malt, hops, yeast, and even name and packaging they wanted used in the company's Beer Rock project. BrewDog released the resulting beer, a black lager named Zeitgeist, in May 2009.

Talk to people involved with beer, whether they are brewers, ad people, marketers, or even historians who study drink, and they'll talk about the intense personal relationship that people develop with what's in their glass. Something they find hard to put into words. Or that they are reluctant to talk about. For decades, the relationship Canadians had with beer was like a hopeless high school crush. We loved it with all our heart and soul; it acted as if we didn't exist. With the birth of the micros, Canadian beer started to love us back.

Brew pubs and other bars dedicated largely to beer have sprung up across Canada.

THROUGH A GLASS, LIQUIDLY

PERHAPS I AM uniquely blessed with a beer-etic memory, but I swear I can still remember my first sip of beer. It was from a warm, almost empty stubby that my parents or their friends had left out on the porch at the cottage. I tipped it into my mouth and a wondrous, flat fluid hit my taste buds—the bitterest thing I had ever tasted. I've talked to other people about this and we all agree: that early flavour stays with you, and it is difficult to find it again. (Though there is a bit of an echo of it in later life: the first sip of the first beer of the day is always better than the last slug from the tenth or eleventh, which I guess is a good thing.)

My next memorable experience with beer was when I went to university. And although beer then didn't have that mystic oomph of those long-ago stubbies (it always seemed to be Blue in those days), it certainly served to make other people more interesting, which is one of beer's

< *Just one letter separates beer and bear. Coincidence? You decide.*

greatest properties. Happily, by the time I was in my late twenties and early thirties, and starting to develop something like taste, the country was in the early stages of the microbrewing revolution.

Thinking about my own experiences has helped me to understand why beer has the status it has. It's not just that it was easy to make in the Canada of our ancestors (so was pemmican, but you don't see it around much today). Or that it embodies some ideal essence of Canadianness (usually conceived of as some sort of down-home earnestness.) No, it is something else. A relatively simple fluid, beer is protean. It

Whatever we are or become, different beers (above) arise to meet the challenge.

can change as we do. When we were simple farm folk, we drank simple farm folk beer. When we became a nation of factory hands and office clerks, beer changed with us. When we'd won the war and were living in the affluent mass society of the 1950s, we had mass beer to go with that shift. When the dominant sensibility of post-industrial Canada became the knowledgeable

hyper-fussy consumer, we developed beers to match that change. Sure it might be fun to have a beverage that is totally, uniquely Canadian (some sort of fermented muskox milk would probably do the trick), but would it have the flexibility and adaptability of beer? Could you drink it sitting on the end of a dock? And where does it say that something has to be native to a country to help define it? Baseball probably defines the United States. Well, baseball is just the English game of rounders on steroids. And what is more British today than chicken tikka? In a nation of immigrants it doesn't matter where you started from but what you do once you get here. And beer became our defining drink. Not everyone drinks it, not everyone has to—no more than every last Frenchman has to wear a beret and eat snails. But we should acknowledge it. It deserves our respect, even our love.

Above all, though, it deserves to be drunk.

Paradise is within sight. Go ahead, get wet.

ACKNOWLEDGEMENTS

Writing *Brew North* was like a dream come true for me—a project I'd thought about for years. But I could never have done it on my own. A lot of people helped me make it happen.

Thanks first of all to Larry Sherk, without doubt Canada's greatest collector of breweriana, the happy name given the riotous assemblage of bottles, posters, mirrors, ashtrays, and what-have-you that Canadian brewers have pumped out over the last hundred-plus years. When first hunting for material to include in this book, every collector said the same thing: "I don't have anything Larry doesn't have." Larry welcomed me into his home and made his extensive collection available. More than a collector, Larry is also an avid historian of beer in Canada, and he read this manuscript for accuracy. I must also thank Joel Manning, brewmaster at Toronto's Mill Street Brewery, for explaining the ins and outs of brewing to me and checking what I wrote on the subject. Thanks, too, to my third expert reader, Ian Bowering, who has forgotten more about the history of beer than I will ever know. Ian also provided me with many hard-to-find photographs. Lots of other enthusiasts helped me with this book. Four in particular deserve mention: Loren Newman, Pat Hunter, Allan Dodd (possessor of Kingston's, if not Canada's, most extensive collection of stubbies), and the late Richard Sweet. Any mistakes that appear in this book are mine, not theirs.

The work of Ian Brewster, my unflappable, affable, and always professional photographer contributed so much to the look of this book. Thank you.

In the brewing industry, I would like particularly to thank Steve Abrams of Mill Street and Sybil Taylor of Steam Whistle. My gratitude also goes to Nellie Swart, the archivist at Labatt in London, who got me in pretty much the day before their old ads and photos were sent off to the University of Western Ontario. In the advertising and marketing sphere, thanks to Doug Linton, Glen Hunt (creator of the famed Molson "Rant"), and David Kincaid. Thanks to Frank Appleton, father of microbrewing in Canada, for permission to quote from his seminal *Harrowsmith* article. Thanks also to Phil Dunning of Parks Canada for answering numerous technical questions about beer dispensing.

Greystone Books—in particular, Rob Sanders, Nancy Flight, and Carra Simpson—have provided great support. On the editorial side I'd like to thank my great editor, Susan Folkins, Pam Robertson, who copy-edited this manuscript, and Ruth Gaskill, who did the proofreading, as well as Jessica Hum-Antonopoulos, who put together the bibliography.

Finally, thanks as always to my wife, Catharine Lyons-King. Catharine worked the scanner, styled photos, created the index, acted as my first reader, and, probably most important of all, dreamed up the title for this dream book.

PHOTO CREDITS

Every effort has been made to correctly identify and credit the copyright holders of the illustrations used in Brew North. *Any oversights or errors will be corrected in subsequent editions.*

FACING 1. Library and Archives Canada, PA 80920. 2. TOP: Sleeman Breweries Limited. INSET: Lawrence Sherk Collection. 3. Lawrence Sherk Collection. 4. Film Reference Library, Toronto International Film Festival Group. 5. BOTH: Lawrence Sherk Collection. 6. Labatt Brewing Company Limited fonds, The University of Western Ontario Archives. 8. Library and Archives Canada, C 089660. 9. Lawrence Sherk Collection. 10. Toronto Public Library. 11. TOP: Molson Coors Canada Archives. BOTTOM: Molson Archives Collection, Library and Archives Canada, PA 125228. 12. Mary Evans Picture Library, 10053953. 13. Ian Bowering Collection. 14. Labatt Brewing Company Limited fonds, The University of Western Ontario Archives. 15. Lawrence Sherk Collection. 16. LEFT: Ian Bowering Collection. RIGHT: Labatt Brewing Company Limited fonds, The University of Western Ontario Archives. 17. Labatt Brewing Company Limited fonds, The University of Western Ontario Archives. 18. Anheuser-Busch. 19. Anheuser-Busch. 20. Lawrence Sherk Collection. Photograph by Ian Brewster. 21. Library and Archives Canada, e 000756699. 22. TOP: Moosehead Breweries Limited. BOTTOM: Sleeman Breweries Limited. 23. BOTH: Lawrence Sherk Collection. 24. Library and Archives Canada, PA 178789. 26. Toronto Public Library, JRR 1412. 27. ALL: Lawrence Sherk Collection. 28. TOP: Molson Archives Collection, Library and Archives Canada, e 008300580. BOTTOM: Glenbow Archives, NA-1280-14. 29. Toronto Public Library, JRR 716. 30. Kingston Brewing Company. 31. Molson Archives Collection, Library and Archives Canada, PA 117556. 32. Molson Archives Collection, Library and Archives Canada, PA 139492. 33. Lawrence Sherk Collection. 34. Library and Archives Canada, NL 008707. 35. TOP: Lawrence Sherk Collection. BOTTOM: Glenbow Archives, NA-3903-28. 36. Lawrence Sherk Collection. Photograph by Ian Brewster. 37. Lawrence Sherk Collection. 38. Lawrence Sherk Collection. 39. Lawrence Sherk Collection. 40. BOTH: Lawrence Sherk Collection. Photographs by Ian Brewster. 41. Lawrence Sherk Collection. Photograph by Ian Brewster. 42. Labatt Brewing Company Limited fonds, The University of Western Ontario Archives. 43. Labatt Brewing Company Limited fonds, The University of Western Ontario Archives. 44. TOP LEFT AND RIGHT: Lawrence Sherk Collection. BOTTOM: Library and Archives Canada, PA 107328. 45. Library and Archives Canada, a 125765. 46. BOTH: Lawrence Sherk Collection. 47. BOTH: Lawrence Sherk Collection. 48. Library and Archives Canada, a 069901. 50. Library and Archives Canada, e 008300582. 51. Lawrence Sherk Collection. 52. Library and Archives Canada, e 008300581. 53. LEFT: Molson Archives Collection, Library and Archives Canada, e 008300587. RIGHT: Molson Archives Collection, Library and Archives Canada, e 008300588. 54. LEFT: Glenbow Archives, NA-1639-2. RIGHT: Glenbow Archives, NA-3509-8. 55. Library and Archives Canada, a 022720. 56. Library and Archives Canada, a 069965. 57. Lawrence Sherk Collection. 58. Library and Archives Canada, e 008748941-v8. 59. BOTH: Lawrence Sherk Collection. 60. Lawrence Sherk Collection. 61. BOTH: Lawrence Sherk Collection. 62. Lawrence Sherk Collection. 63. Moosehead Breweries Limited.

64. York University Libraries, Clara Thomas Archives & Special Collections, Toronto Telegram fonds, 1821. 66. LEFT: Labatt Brewing Company Limited fonds, The University of Western Ontario Archives. RIGHT, TOP: Ian Bowering Collection. RIGHT, BOTTOM: Labatt Brewing Company Limited fonds, The University of Western Ontario Archives. 67. Lawrence Sherk Collection. 68. Archives of Ontario, I 0041367. 69. Archives of Ontario, I 0041369. 70. TOP: Library and Archives Canada, Bruce Moss, *Weekend* magazine collection, e 008300700. BOTTOM: Lawrence Sherk Collection. Photograph by Ian Brewster. 71. Glenbow Archives, NA-4476-520. 73. York University Libraries, Clara Thomas Archives & Special Collections, Toronto Telegram fonds, ASCO5115. 74. TOP: Library and Archives Canada, PA 113191. BOTTOM: Glenbow Archives, NA-3271-11. 75. Lawrence Sherk Collection. 76. Lawrence Sherk Collection. 77. Library and Archives Canada, PA 150436. 78. Library and Archives Canada, 132059. 80. Lawrence Sherk Collection. Photographs by Ian Brewster. 81. York University Libraries, Clara Thomas Archives & Special Collections, Toronto Telegram fonds, ASCO5119. 82. Lawrence Sherk Collection. 83. Lawrence Sherk Collection. 84. Lawrence Sherk Collection. 85. Lawrence Sherk Collection. 86. Lawrence Sherk Collection. 87. Lawrence Sherk Collection. Photograph by Ian Brewster. 88. Lawrence Sherk Collection. Photograph by Ian Brewster. 89. York University Libraries, Clara Thomas Archives & Special Collections, Toronto Telegram fonds, 1820. 90. BOTH: Lawrence Sherk Collection. 91. BOTH: Ian Bowering Collection. 92. TOP: Library and Archives Canada, PA 108218. BOTTOM: Labatt Brewing Company Limited fonds, The University of Western Ontario Archives. 93. LEFT: Lawrence Sherk Collection. RIGHT: Lawrence Sherk Collection. Photograph by Ian Brewster. 94. LEFT: Labatt Brewing Company Limited fonds, The University of Western Ontario Archives. RIGHT: Lawrence Sherk Collection. 95. LEFT: Moosehead Breweries Limited. RIGHT: Lawrence Sherk Collection. Photograph by Ian Brewster. 96. Associated Screen News, Molson Archives Collection, Library and Archives Canada, PA 119421. 98. Library and Archives Canada, PA 139489. 99. Lawrence Sherk Collection. 100. Lawrence Sherk Collection. 101. Glenbow Archives NB-16-396. 102. Ian Bowering Collection. 103. Ian Bowering Collection. 104. Lawrence Sherk Collection. 105. TOP: Lawrence Sherk Collection. BOTTOM: Lawrence Sherk Collection. Photograph by Ian Brewster. 106. LEFT: Lawrence Sherk Collection. RIGHT: Labatt Brewing Company Limited fonds, The University of Western Ontario Archives. 107. BOTH: Labatt Brewing Company Limited fonds, The University of Western Ontario Archives. 108. Lawrence Sherk Collection. 109. BOTH: Labatt Brewing Company Limited fonds, The University of Western Ontario Archives. 110. Labatt Brewing Company Limited fonds, The University of Western Ontario Archives. 111. Labatt Brewing Company Limited fonds, The University of Western Ontario Archives. 112. BOTH: Labatt Brewing Company Limited fonds, The University of Western Ontario Archives. 113. Lawrence Sherk Collection. 114. York University Libraries, Clara Thomas Archives & Special Collections, Toronto Telegram fonds, ASCO6310. 116. BOTH: Lawrence Sherk Collection. 117. Lawrence Sherk Collection. 118–119. Rick Ambrozic Collection. 120. Lawrence Sherk Collection. 121. BOTH: Lawrence Sherk Collection. 122. LEFT: Labatt Brewing Company Limited fonds, The University of Western Ontario Archives. RIGHT: Lawrence Sherk Collection. 123. BOTH: Lawrence Sherk Collection. 124. BOTH: Lawrence Sherk Collection. 125. BOTH: Lawrence Sherk Collection. 126. Labatt Brewing Company Limited fonds, The University of Western Ontario Archives. 127. Labatt Brewing Company Limited fonds, The University of Western Ontario Archives. 128. Moosehead Breweries Limited. 129. ALL: Moosehead Breweries Limited. 130. Lawrence Sherk Collection. 131. Lawrence Sherk Collection. 132. Corbis/Reuters, DWF15-818846. 133. Lawrence Sherk Collection. 134. Anchor Brewing Company. 136. Frank Appleton. 137. Campaign for Real Ale (CAMRA). 138. TOP: Anchor Brewing Company. BOTTOM: John Mitchell. 139. John Mitchell. 140. BOTH: Granville Island Brewing. 141. Big Rock Brewery. 142. Mill Street Brewery. 143. Alexander Keith's. 144. TOP: Sleeman Breweries Limited. BOTTOM: Big Rock Brewery. 145. Sleeman Breweries Limited. 146. Labatt Brewing Company Limited fonds, The University of Western Ontario Archives. 147. Labatt Brewing Company Limited fonds, The University of Western Ontario Archives. 148. Lawrence Sherk Collection. 149. LEFT: Unibroue inc. RIGHT: Lawrence Sherk Collection. 150. LEFT: Beau's All Natural Brewing Company. RIGHT: Lawrence Sherk Collection. 151. TOP: Wellington County Brewery Incorporated. MIDDLE AND BOTTOM: Picaroons Brewing Company. 152. Steam Whistle Brewing. 153. Quidi Vidi Brewing Company. 154. Creemore Springs Brewery. 155. TOP: Corbis, 42-20372301. BOTTOM: Photograph by Stephen Gardiner. 156. Glenbow Archive, NA-884-3. 157. TOP: Lawrence Sherk Collection. Photograph by Ian Brewster. BOTTOM: Glenbow Archive, NA-3691-20. 158. Lawrence Sherk Collection.

BIBLIOGRAPHY

Appleton, Frank. "The Underground Brewmaster." *Harrowsmith* 13, no. 3,
  (May/June 1978): pp. 84–97.

Beaumont, Stephen. "The Beer Essentials for Lighter Brews: Strong Body, Lots of Taste."
  Globe and Mail, December 13, 2008. http://www.theglobeandmail.com/servlet/story/
  LAC.20081213.BEER13/TPStory/Entertainment (accessed December 17, 2008).

——. *The Great Canadian Beer Guide.* Rev. ed. Toronto: McArthur & Company, 2001.

——. "A Little Beer Goes a Long Way." *Canadian Business,* July 1996,
  pp. 54–59.

Blocker Jr., Jack S., David M. Fahey, and Ian Tyrrell, eds. *Alcohol and Temperance in
  Modern History: An International Encyclopedia.* Santa Barbara: ABC-CLIO, Inc., 2003.

Bloom, Richard. "So You Want To Be a Brewer." *Globe and Mail,* July 24, 2004.
  http://www.theglobeandmail.com/series/business/sb2/globe/08172004b.html
  (accessed May 9, 2009).

Bowering, Ian. *The Art and Mystery of Brewing in Ontario.* Burnstown, ON: General Store
  Publishing, 1988.

——. *Brewing in Formosa: 125 Years of Tradition.* Burnstown, ON: General Store
  Publishing, 1995.

Brent, Paul. *Lager Heads: Labatt, Molson and the People Who Created Canada's Beer Wars.*
  Rev. ed. Toronto: HarperCollins, 2005.

Brewers Association of Canada. *Brewing in Canada.* Ottawa: Brewers Association of
  Canada, 1965.

——. *Supplement to Brewing in Canada.* Ottawa: Brewers Association of Canada, 1967.

Brown, Pete. *Man Walks into a Pub: A Sociable History of Beer.* London: Macmillan, 2003.

Campbell, Robert A. *Sit Down and Drink Your Beer: Regulating Vancouver's Beer Parlours,
  1925–1954.* Toronto: University of Toronto Press, 2001.

Canadian Business. "Sounds Awful, Sells Great." December 1995, p. 78.

Canadian Press. "Sapporo to Buy Sleeman Brewery in $400M Deal." *ctvglobemedia.com*, August 11, 2006. http://www.ctv.ca/servlet/ArticleNews/print/CTVNews/20060811/ sapporo_sleeman (accessed December 1, 2008).

Canadian Press NewsWire. "Microbrew Market Not So Micro." August 2, 1996. http://proquest.umi.com.ezproxy.torontopubliclibrary.ca/pdqweb?did=4188552681&sid =2&Fmt=3&clientld=1525&RQT=309&VNAME=PQD (accessed April 25, 2009).

Canwest News Service. "N.B. Brew Launch Leaves Bad Taste for Some." March 12, 2009. http://proquest.umi.com.ezproxy.torontopubliclibrary.ca/pdqweb?did=166137025&sid=1 &Fmt=3&clientld=1525&RQT=309&VName=PQD (accessed May 8, 2009).

cbc News. "Alcohol: By the Numbers." October 15, 2008. http://www.cbc.ca/canada/ story/2008/10/10/f-alcohol-numbers.html (accessed July 7, 2009).

——— . "Molson Shareholders Approve Coors Merger." January 28, 2005. http://www.cbc.ca/money/story/2005/01/28/molson-050128.html (accessed November 5, 2008).

Clow, Meribeth, Dorothy Duncan, Glenn J. Lockwood, and Lorraine Lowry, eds. *Consuming Passions: Eating and Drinking Traditions in Ontario*. Willowdale, ON: Ontario Historical Society, 1990.

cnn Money. "Coors, Molson Brew a Merger." July 22, 2004. http://money.cnn.com/2004/07/22/news/fortune500/coors_molson (accessed November 5, 2008).

Decarie, Graeme. "Paved with Good Intentions: The Prohibitionists' Road to Racism in Ontario." *Ontario History* 66, no. 1 (March 1974): pp. 15 22.

DeCloet, Derek. "Trouble Brewing in Beer Industry." *ctvglobemedia.com*. May 7, 2005. http://gold.globeinvestor.com/servlet/story/LAC.20050507.RCOVER07/APStory/?query (accessed May 9, 2009).

DeLottinville, Peter. "Joe Beef of Montreal: Working Class Culture and the Tavern, 1869–1889." *Labour/Le Travail* 8-9 (Autumn 1981/Spring 1982): pp. 9–40.

Denison, Merrill. *The Barley and the Stream: The Molson Story*. Toronto: McClelland & Stewart, 1955.

Dick, Ernest J. "From Temperance to Prohibition in 19th Century Nova Scotia." *Dalhousie Review* 61, no. 3 (Autumn 1981): pp. 530–52.

D'Innocenzo, Lisa. "50 Years of Labatt Blue: Timeline." *Strategy Magazine*, October 2006. http://www.strategymag.com/articles/magazine/20061001/bluetimeline.html (accessed March 3, 2009).

Dominion Brewers Association. *Facts on the Brewing Industry in Canada, a National Industry: A Manual Outlining the Development of the Industry and Its Place in the Canadian Economy*. Ottawa: Dominion Brewers Association, 1948.

Economist. "A Heady Start." August 26, 1995, p. 57.

Edmonton Journal. "Canadians Cheer Red Wine and Beer: Statscan." April 21, 2009, p. A5.

Faulkner, Douglas. "The Brand Builder: How Grandad's Little Black Book Made John Sleeman's Microbrewery a Macro Player in the Premium Beer Market." *Canadian Packaging* 50, no. 3 (March 1997): p. 15.

Ferguson, Rob. "Molson Increases Stake in Microbrewery." Canadian Press NewsWire, May 12, 1997. http://proquest.umi.com.ezproxy.torontopubliclibrary.ca/pqdweb?did=404873091&sid=2&Fmt=3&clientld=1525&RQT=309&VName=PQD (accessed April 25, 2009).

Fillion, Roger. "Feds Give Nod to Molson Coors, Miller Merger." *Rocky Mountain News,* June 5, 2008. http://www.rockymountainnews.com/news/2008/jun/05/feds-clear-joint-venture-brewers/ (accessed November 5, 2008).

Gray, James H. *Bacchanalia Revisited: Western Canada's Boozy Skid to Social Disaster.* Saskatoon, SK: Western Producer Prairie Books, 1982.

——. *Booze: The Impact of Whisky on the Prairie West.* Scarborough, ON: New American Library of Canada, 1972.

Guillet, Edwin C. *Pioneer Inns and Taverns.* Toronto: Ontario Publishing Company, 1964.

Haliburton, G. Brenton. *What's Brewing: Oland, 1867–1971; A History.* Tantallon, NS: Four East Publications, 1994.

Heron, Craig. *Booze: A Distilled History.* Toronto: Between the Lines, 2003.

——. "The Boys and Their Booze: Masculinities and Public Drinking in Working-Class Hamilton, 1880–1946." Paper presented to the North American Labor History Conference, Detroit, 2002.

Holloway, Andy. "A Tall Order." *Canadian Business*, May 13, 2002, pp. 29–31.

Hughes, Jeanne. "Inns and Taverns." In Clow et al., eds., *Consuming Passions*, pp. 93–112.

Hunter, Douglas. *Molson: The Birth of a Business Empire.* Toronto: Penguin, 2001.

Hunter, Patrick J. "The 'Stubby' in Canada: A Compact History." In *Bottoms Up! Spirited Reflections on Drinking in Canada*, edited by Christine Sismondo, Heather Siemens, and Amanda McFillen. Toronto: Museum Studies Program, University of Toronto, 2007.

Jackson, Michael. *Michael Jackson's Beer Companion.* Don Mills, ON: General Publishing, 1993.

Jenish, D'Arcy. "Go Public or Stay Private?" *ctvglobemedia.com*, October 7, 2004. http://gold.globeinvestor.com/servlet/story/LAC.20041007.ROSBPUBLIC/APStory/?query (accessed May 9, 2009).

Jorgensen, Bud. "Snobbish Stocking Stuffer for Exec with Everything." *Globe and Mail*, December 23, 1987, p. B5.

Kingsmill, David. "'David' Opens New Brewery as Big Goliath Goes Aussie." *Toronto Star*, April 2, 1986, p. B5.

Lawrason, David. "Canadian Beer Market Going Flat." *Globe and Mail*, July 18, 1987, p. C14.

Lazarus, Eve. "Granville at New Stage in 'Beer Life.'" *Marketing Magazine*, June 24, 2002, p. 4.

———. "Granville Island Brewing Renaming Beer Brands." *Marketing Magazine,* June 2, 1997, p. 4.

Leacock, Stephen. "The Tyranny of Prohibition." In *The Social Criticism of Stephen Leacock: The Unsolved Riddle of Social Justice and Other Essays,* edited by Alan Bowker, pp. 61–69. Toronto: University of Toronto Press, 1973.

Leary, Mike. "Cottage Brewers Tap Into Growing Specialty Markets." *Toronto Star,* October 14, 1983, p. B4.

Lem, Sharon. "Got Our Beer Goggles On." *Toronto Sun,* April 21, 2009, p. 3.

Lockwood, Glenn J. "Music and Songs Related to Food and Beverages." In Clow et al., eds., *Consuming Passions,* pp. 233–37.

———. "Temperance in Upper Canada as Ethnic Subterfuge." In *Drink in Canada: Historical Essays,* edited by Cheryl Krasnick Warsh, pp. 43–69. Montreal: McGill-Queen's University Press, 1993.

Love, Myron. "Struggling Microbreweries Join Forces." *Food in Canada*, March 2003, p. 10.

MacDonald, Jason. "Full Steam Ahead." *Canadian Packaging,* September 2000, p. 50.

Mah, Bill. "Global Hop Shortage Giving Microbrews the Blues." *Edmonton Journal,* November 21, 2007, p. 1.

Maich, Steve. "Molson to Merge with Coors." *The Canadian Encyclopedia Historica,* August 2, 2004. http://www.thecanadianencyclopedia.com/PrinterFriendly. cfm?Params=M1ARTM0012633 (accessed November 5, 2008).

Malleck, Daniel J. "Priorities of Development in Four Local Women's Christian Temperance Unions in Ontario, 1877–1895." In *Changing Face of Drink: Substance, Imagery and Behaviour,* edited by Jack S. Blocker Jr. and Cheryl Krasnick Warsh, pp. 189–208. Ottawa: Social History Inc., c. 1977.

Marquis, Greg. "Civilized Drinking: Alcohol and Society in New Brunswick, 1945–1975." *Journal of the Canadian Historical Society,* 2000, pp. 173–203.

Martin, Robert. "All Hail—It's Real Ale!" *Globe and Mail,* May 26, 1984, p. 12.

Maurer, Harry, and Christina Lindblad. "Brewers in One Bottle." *Business Week,* October 22, 2007. http://find.galegroup.com.ezproxy.torontopubliclibrary.ca/itx/start. do?prodId=EAIM (accessed November 5, 2008).

McBurney, Margaret, and Mary Byers. *Tavern in the Town: Early Inns and Taverns of Ontario.* Toronto: University of Toronto Press, 1987.

McGovern, Cynthia. "The Best-Laid Plans: Despite Careful Research and Planning, Gary Hoeschen Encountered Plenty of Pitfalls on the Road to Launching Manitoba's First Microbrewery." *Profit,* October 1, 1995, p. 117.

Merritt, Richard D. "Early Inns and Taverns: Accommodation, Fellowship, and Good Cheer." In *Capital Years: Niagara-on-the-Lake, 1792–1796,* edited by Richard Merritt, Nancy Butler, and Michael Power, pp. 187–222. Toronto: Dundurn Press, 1991.

Ministry of Finance (Ontario). "Province Simplifies Brewers' Basic Fee to Benefit Small Brewers." Government press release, August 31, 2001. http://proquest.umi.com.ezproxy. torontopubliclibrary.ca/pqdweb?did=79259193&sid=1&Fmt=3&clientld=1525&RQT=30 9&VName=PQD (accessed April 25, 2009).

Molson, Karen. *The Molsons: Their Lives and Times, 1780–2000*. Toronto: Firefly Books, 2001.

Motherwell, Cathryn. "Small Brewers Find it Hard to Get Ahead." *Globe and Mail*, February 17, 1986, p. B3.

Novak, Phil. "Ad Execs Have Hand in Brewery Revival." *Marketing Magazine*, June 29, 1998, p. 10.

Ogle, Maureen. *Ambitious Brew: The Story of American Beer*. Orlando, FL: Harcourt, 2006.

Ontario Craft Brewers. "Canadian Craft Brewers Applaud Cut to Excise Duty in Federal Budget." News on Tap (assocation press release), May 3, 2006. http://www.ontariocraftbrewers.com/content2.php?nextpage=ocb_press_release_may3_06 (accessed May 12, 2009).

Papoff, Lawrence. "Last Call for a Crafty Rebel." *Profit*, September 1, 1998, p. 31.

Partridge, John. "Would-be Brewers Seek Market Access." *Globe and Mail*, September 1, 1984, pp. B1–B2.

Pitts, Gordon. "A New Beer Baron, and His Take on Liquid Assets." *Globe and Mail*, September 29, 2008, p. B1.

Restrictive Trades Practices Commission. *Report Concerning an Alleged Combine in the Manufacture, Distribution and Sale of Beer in Canada*. Ottawa: Queen's Printer, 1955.

Roberts, H. Julia. "Harry Jones and His Cronies in the Taverns of Kingston, Canada West." *Ontario History* 95, no. 1 (Spring 2003): pp. 1–21.

——. "Taverns and Tavern-goers in Upper Canada, the 1790s to the 1850s." PhD diss., University of Toronto, 1999.

Rohmer, Richard. *E.P. Taylor: The Biography of Edward Plunket Taylor*. Toronto: McClelland & Stewart, 1978.

Sawler, Harvey. *Last Canadian Beer: The Moosehead Story*. Halifax, NS: Nimbus Publishing, c. 2008.

Shea, Albert A. *Vision in Action: The Story of Canadian Breweries Limited from 1930 to 1955*. Toronto: Canadian Breweries, 1955.

Smale, Will. "What Exactly Is In Your Beer?" *BBC News*. May 1, 2006. http://news.bbc.co.uk/go/pr/fr/-/2/hi/business/4942262.stm (accessed July 28, 2009).

Smart, Reginald G., and Alan C. Ogborne. *Northern Spirits: A Social History of Alcohol in Canada*. Toronto: Addiction Research Foundation, 1996.

Sneath, Allen Winn. *Brewed in Canada: The Untold Story of Canada's 350-Year-Old Brewing Industry*. Toronto: Dundurn Group, 2001.

Strauss, Marina. "What Happened to Blue." *Globe and Mail*, February 21, 2008, p. B1.

Sturgis, J.L. "'The Spectre of a Drunkard's Grave': One Family's Battle with Alcohol in Late Nineteenth-Century Canada." In *Drink in Canada: Historical Essays,* edited by Cheryl Krasnick Warsh, pp. 115–43. Montreal: McGill-Queen's University Press, 1993.

Summerfield, Patti. "Molson Launches Old-style Beers." *Strategy Magazine*, November 29, 1993. http://www.strategymag.com/articles/magazine/19931129/8074.html (accessed November 5, 2009).

Sweet, Richard L. *The Directory of Canadian Breweries (Past and Present)*. 2nd ed. Saskatoon: Self-published, 1996.

Tenszen, Michael. "The Brew Pub Goes Down Well." *Globe and Mail*, July 19, 1984, p. 8.

Trading Markets. "Regulators Sign Off on Miller, Coors Merger." June 5, 2008. http://www.tradingmarkets.com/print.site/news/Stock%20News/1663645/ (accessed November 5, 2008).

Tucker, Albert. "Labatt's: A History—From Immigrant Family to Canadian Corporation." Unpublished manuscript.

Unibroue Brewery. "Unibroue—A U Beer to Celebrate." Corporate press release, June 25, 1999. http://proquest.umi.com.ezproxy.torontopubliclibrary.ca/pqdweb?did=42699707 &sid=1&Fmt=3&clicntld=1525&RQT=309&VName=PQD (accessed April 25, 2009).

Waal, Peter. "Molson Muscle?" *Canadian Business*, July 31, 1998, p. 18.

Western Report. "Tears in Their Beers: The Drummond Brewing Collapse Sours the Alberta Pool." August 28, 1995, p. 15.

INDEX

172

IAN COUTTS is the author of several books, including *Titanic: The Last Great Images* (with Robert Ballard) and *The Ultimate Guys' Q & A* (released in the United States as *Do Nymphomaniacs Really Exist?*). He divides his time among Toronto; Kingston, Ontario; and Merida, Mexico. www.couttsandking.com